The
EXTRAORDINARY
MILLIONAIRE

The
EXTRAORDINARY
MILLIONAIRE

Harness the REAL tools for success, grow your wealth and build an extraordinary life

NICHOLAS WALLWORK

Contents

About the Author

Nicholas Wallwork is a multi-millionaire property investor, developer, International For Dummies author, and accredited property educator and mentor. Well-known for his role on SKY TV as a property investment angel on Property Elevator, Nicholas has a highly respected name within the property sector and regularly appears as a property market commentator on TV, YouTube, podcasts, radio and at national property events.

Nicholas fell into property in 2002 when he realised turning his first house into a small HMO (rather than living in it himself) made complete financial sense. HMOs and commercial-to-residential development were to form key strategies of his successful property career. Aged just 25 he had no mortgage or bills to pay and could effectively retire (albeit modestly), teaching him a very early lesson that passive income from assets (property and investments) was the way to build long term wealth and a flexible, comfortable and happy lifestyle.

Today, Nicholas has developed in excess of £100million worth of UK property and is an owner in a group of successful property businesses, Redbrick, including a property investment consultancy, several development companies, and a lettings and management business. True wealth starts in the mind. It crystalises purpose and passion, it becomes a way of life, it enables freedom, it encourages compassion, and it ensures legacy.

Any journey through life (and indeed property) is never plain sailing and Nicholas definitely faced his share of challenges. Surviving the credit crunch and Covid were some of the biggest, teaching him many important lessons which he shares with you through The Extraordinary Millionaire books and live online courses, and his 1-2-1 mentorships. To be successful in any business including property you need to stay at the top of your game. This means continually educating yourself and improving your skills and knowledge to further your business and personal success.

CONNECT WITH ME

As you work your way through this book, I'd love to hear what you think. Which tools and techniques really resonated with you? Did some of them surprise you? What bits made you sit up and say 'Yes! That's so true.'

You can connect with me on Instagram (I'm **@nicholas_wallwork**), on LinkedIn, and via my websites **www.extraordinarymillionaire.com** and **www.nicholaswallwork.com**. I can't wait to hear from you!

Dedication

This book is dedicated to my soul mate and amazing wife, Britta Wallwork, and to my amazing, always positive family Siènna, Skyla, and Silàs. Thank you, Britta, for believing in me always and without question, right from the outset. We will always dream big and continue to enjoy every moment as though it's our last.

Author's Acknowledgments

A big thank you to my fellow directors at Redbrick and my whole team for helping us deliver our unique development projects. I'd also like to thank our extended project management team and trusted 'power team' consultants who we work with across our various companies, without whom we would not be able to produce the results for our clients that we do.

On a personal note, I'd like to send my deep gratitude and heartfelt thanks to Salarah who has been my own life coach for over a decade now. She has help me hone my own mindset when I needed it most. She's re-aligned me notably on two occasions when I had run out of my own tools in my toolkit and she's a powerhouse of mindset & law of attraction knowledge and insanely talented life coach. Whether I've been looking to fine tune myself at peak performance or help me get out of a rut, when I've turned to her for guidance she has always inspired me and helped me level up to the next level.

Thank you to all my Joint Venture partners, personal 1-2-1 mentees for your support and engagement as you all embark on your own wealth creation journeys. I'm grateful to have been able to help so many people achieve so much and seeing you do well is one of my biggest goals in life. Onwards and upwards!

A final thank you to all our JV partners and investors who have trusted us through both the good and tough times in the market allowing us to continue to push forward creating win/win relationships in everything that we do and moving from strength to strength.

Consultations with Nicholas

Nicholas is passionate about helping others succeed in property and offers tailored 1-2-1 consultation sessions to help people fast-track their property investment goals and make real progress. He can help you make key decisions on maximising layout and value from a property, overcome issues with planning, secure the right finance structure for your project, make the jump to larger more complex developments, move into a different strategy completely, attract private investors, navigate the construction and post-construction phases, and successfully market your finished product.

Link to Consultation Packages: **www.nicholaswallwork.com**

ALSO BY NICHOLAS WALLWORK

The Rock Bottom
Paradox

Professional Property
Strategies

Advanced Property
Development

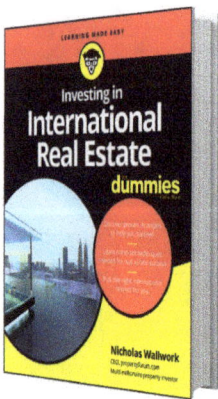

Investing In International
Real Estate **For Dummies**

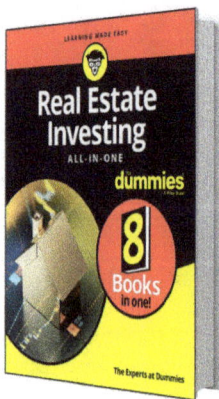

Real Estate Investing
(All-In-One) **For Dummies**

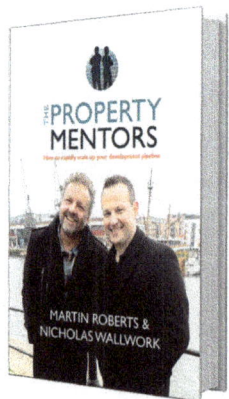

The Property
Mentors

Introduction

I was a millionaire in my head long before I actually became one on paper. I lived with abundance and wealth in mind, instead of focusing on all the things I didn't have. I told myself I was successful even when (in the early days) I was scraping by. I lived, breathed and acted the part of an Extraordinary Millionaire until I was one for real.

WHAT IS AN EXTRAORDINARY MILLIONAIRE?

An Extraordinary Millionaire is someone who focuses on abundance, not just money. Because, let's be honest, you can be stinking rich and still never feel like you have enough. Maybe you know someone like that already - someone who seemingly has everything a person could ever wish for and yet it's not enough for them. They're always looking at the grass on the other side of the fence to see if it's greener than theirs. That's not an Extraordinary Millionaire.

An Extraordinary Millionaire is someone who gives thanks for the life they have, while striving for the life they want. Someone who knows that mindset plays an enormous role in success, and shapes their thoughts accordingly. Someone who is continually learning, rather than kidding themselves that they know everything. Someone who has unlearned the harmful lessons about money that hold so many people back from a life of abundance. Someone who knows how to make money work *for them*, instead of working for money. Someone who builds mutually beneficial business relationships instead of pushing others down. Someone who gives back.

The path of an Extraordinary Millionaire certainly isn't the only path to wealth, success and abundance. But it's the only path I want to take. I wouldn't want to be successful any other way. Because I believe that we get back what we put out there. As such, the best way to build multi-generational wealth and freedom for myself and my loved ones is to raise myself up, while also raising up those around me. And that includes you.

BUT WHY SHOULD YOU LISTEN TO ME?

Because I've been where you are. I didn't grow up wealthy (comfortable, happy, just not rich). But I knew I wanted to become an Extraordinary Millionaire. I knew that a life working 9 to 5 just to make other people wealthy wasn't for me. Instead, I had a different future in mind, one where I had financial freedom.

So I set myself some salty goals and embarked on a mission of personal development and education. I devoured everything I could get my hands on to do with investing, passive income, property, self-help techniques, autobiographies of entrepreneurs, you name it. Anything that either inspired me to succeed or gave me practical techniques I could work into my daily routine. And I threw myself into the world of property, going to national shows, networking, connecting with potential investing partners, and so on.

I made my first property million within a few years, only to lose most of it in the 2008 financial crash. But strangely, that didn't knock me down. I knew I could get it all back again and more, using my trusty toolkit of techniques. That challenging time also cemented the importance of diversification and passive income, since the rental portion of my property portfolio really saved my bacon during that period. I learned a lot - and as you'll see in this book, when you're learning, you're not failing!

Fast-forward a few years and I've built a multi-million-pound property portfolio, spanning several real estate businesses, including the largest international property forum, propertyforum.com. I've always been passionate about educating myself, but through the forum, I became passionate about educating other budding investors. Which is how I began working as a property mentor, TV presenter and an author in the renowned *For Dummies* series.

I've always been fascinated by the habits of successful people, which is partly why I'm a business book junkie. Thanks to this voracious reading appetite, I have, over many years, accumulated a range of success-boosting mindset and business-related habits that have made a huge difference to both my outlook and my business results. Those regular habits spawned this book. I wanted to write something that pulled a range of success-boosting tips and techniques into one book - a book that could be devoured in one sitting (if you're a book junkie like me) and revisited time and time again.

WHAT CAN YOU EXPECT FROM THIS BOOK?

This book is a toolkit, basically. It's full of practical tools and tips that have got me where I am today. These techniques are not a shortcut to success (if anyone promises you a shortcut to riches, they're probably about to rip you off). But they will absolutely help you get there. Yes, it'll take hard work, effort and commitment, but the results . . . oh boy, the results are so worth it. Financial and lifestyle freedom (the freedom to work when you want, for example), building a more secure future for yourself and your loved ones, building an abundant life, fulfilling your potential, and showing your children (if you have them) a different path in life than the 'norm'. I could go on, but doesn't that sound good for starters?

My forte is obviously property - and I'd honestly advise any budding investor to get into property - but rest assured these techniques can be applied to building success in any business or industry.

Glancing at the table of contents, you might be surprised to see half of it dedicated to practical mindset techniques and tools for mental strength. Things like meditation, visualisation and positive affirmations. Not only are these tools (in my opinion) vital for building success and wealth, they're useful for managing your mental health. I've had low points in my mental health, and the ability to practise things like mindfulness and visualisation pulled me through. In other words, this toolkit is for the good times and the not-so-good times. Use it to build your wealth. Use it to transform your life. And use it when you just need a shot of positivity and reassurance that you can overcome whatever life throws at you. With these tools up your sleeve, you can.

By the way, for even more of a focus on mental health, you might like to check out my other book, *The Rock Bottom Paradox: A blueprint for turning adversity into opportunity.* It's all about healing, building resilience and overcoming life's challenges. Importantly, it's not just about climbing out from rock bottom and getting back to where you were in life - it's about building something new and exciting for yourself. It is, as the title suggests, about turning adversity into an incredible opportunity.

The tools in this book can also be used with your children to help them build mental resilience, foster a positive mindset and boost their confidence. My wife and I have taught our children to use things like positive affirmations and gratitude because, to us, they're life skills. Whatever path our children choose in life, we believe these techniques will help them build happy, fulfilling lives.

But this book is not just about practical tools. I also wanted it to be inspirational, spurring you on to take your first steps towards becoming an Extraordinary Millionaire. That's why the book has more of a storytelling feel than you might find in other business books. I believe structuring these practical tools around a story allows them to be understood by absolutely anyone, regardless of where you are in life or what sort of business/financial experience you have. And that's where George comes in . . .

WHO THE HELL IS GEORGE?

Every conversation I have with George in this book is a conversation I've had at one time or another with friends, family, acquaintances, or someone I've met along the way. In this way, George is an amalgamation of many people I've known in my life. People who desperately wanted to escape the rat race but lacked the confidence or commitment to invest in their own education and take the practical steps needed. People who thought a life of abundance and financial freedom was beyond their reach.

I'm delighted to say some of these people did ultimately make the transition from Rat Racer to Extraordinary Millionaire. Others ended up staying in their rat race lane, continuing working to make other people rich, continuing to worry about money while accumulating liabilities, and continuing to tell themselves that the rat race is more secure than life as an entrepreneur.

I've learned from both kinds of people. I've learned what makes a Rat Racer tick (especially why they stay put) and I've learned what motivates people to finally break free. You'll find those lessons in these pages, and I hope they resonate with you. I hope George and I inspire you to pull out of the rat race lane and start building your own road to an abundant future.

Is George one of the people who will seize the opportunity and break free? Well, you'll have to read on to find out.

But for now, let's take the initial step towards becoming an Extraordinary Millionaire and pull out the first technique in our toolbox: setting extraordinary goals.

Part I:
The Extraordinary Mindset

TECHNIQUES TO TRANSFORM
YOUR WAY OF THINKING

'Once your mindset changes, everything on the
outside will change along with it.'

–STEVE MARABOLI

Chapter 1

Setting Extraordinary Goals

It started with a zip line. A rickety homemade zip line that my best friend and I strung up in the woodland opposite our family home. Twenty foot in the air, the zip line was attached to a rudimentary rope bridge strung between two trees. We'd climb one tree, shimmy across the rope bridge, then grab onto the zip wire and jump off. Nothing beneath us but air. Nothing above us but the synthetic blue rope that formed our - in hindsight - extremely dubious zip line. We loved it.

'That's what I want for our kids,' I said to my wife. 'A big house and garden with our own little bit of woodland, freedom to roam, and a zip line. A proper one, though.'

She wasn't my wife yet. And I wasn't a millionaire. I had been a millionaire, briefly, before losing almost everything in the 2008 financial crash, when my first property company went bust. Out of a burgeoning property portfolio, I was left with two small rental properties that - once I'd covered the mortgages and bills each month - gave me a tiny passive income. I was scraping by on that, driving a £100 Peugeot 106 with a hole in the passenger side floor, and living in a perfectly ordinary house on a perfectly ordinary street with perfectly ordinary neighbours. Nothing wrong with that, if that lights your fire. But to me it was a stopgap. A stepping stone on the way back to prosperity, and to one day raising a family in the home of our dreams.

I was starting again as an entrepreneur, basically, just as my future wife and I were starting a life together. It was a leap of faith, not unlike when I used to step off into the fresh air and expect that blue rope to hold me. I leapt, believing that I'd rebuild my property business and, not just get back what I'd achieved before, but be even more successful. And she leapt with me.

The neighbour, George, thought I was mad.

'Why don't you just go back to working in the City?' he asked. 'Good money, reliable income. That knackered thing is gonna die any day.'

He meant the Peugeot 106. Not me.

'But that was miserable,' I said. '*I* was miserable.'

'So? It's work. It's not supposed to be fun.'

This is a crucial difference between the mindset of an Extraordinary Millionaire and the Rat Racer mindset that so many of us find ourselves trapped in. To my friend next door, work was about earning money and clawing onto some sense of security.

George was a similar age to me, newly married, first child on the way, and almost a decade into a pretty successful sales career. We bonded over a shared love of music and cars (or, more accurately, I admired his nearly-new BMW and he regularly poked fun at my crappy Peugeot). I liked him, with his dry sense of humour and unvarnished opinions.

But I disagreed with him about work.

'If work is going to take up my precious time, energy and headspace – which it does for everyone, unless you have a 100% passive income – it has to be something I enjoy. Preferably *love*,' I explained.

After all, I knew there was another path. One that diverged from the traditional route of find a steady job, put in those long hours, climb the ladder, and constantly keep looking for the next promotion and pay rise. I knew it because I'd had a taste of it with my previous property company. I suspected George knew it too, deep down. But he also knew that the rat race is a hard thing to turn your back on.

'Sounds great in theory,' he said. 'But I have responsibilities.'

There was another difference between us, beyond our attitude to work. My Rat Racer friend next door had dreams. Whereas I had goals.

WHAT'S THE DIFFERENCE?

George dreamt of owning a better car, achieving a certain level in his sales career, being rich, being happy, taking the kids to Disneyland, and retiring somewhere warm one day.

My goals weren't dissimilar: a fancy car (like I said, I've always been a car nut, but at that point anything would have been better than the Peugeot), a certain level of monthly passive income from property and investments, a little place in the Netherlands, where my wife is from. And, of course, that dream family home in England with a piece of woodland heaven, complete with camp fires and a zip line. Hell, why not a yurt as well?

On paper, then, the Rat Racer and the Extraordinary (Aspiring) Millionaire wanted similar things out of life. So what's the difference between his dreams and my goals?

One difference lies in how we defined our goals. Someone with a Rat Racer mindset pines for general wishes like being rich. (Probably because it's easy to wish for general things. As soon as you start drilling down into specifics, you get scarily close to having to do something.)

'What's wrong with that?' George asked. 'Surely you also want to be rich . . . again,' he added.

'It's not specific enough for me,' I argued. 'A goal should be specific and measurable, right?'

'Go on . . .' George prompted.

'So, rather than just "being rich", I have a specific figure in mind for how much passive income I want to earn each month in order to live an abundant, comfortable life. And, of course, I want to build enough wealth to buy my dream house in a dream setting in the countryside.'

Likewise, rather than just 'being happy', the Extraordinary Millionaire way is to define what 'happiness' looks like. In my case, working for myself and having the freedom to set my own agenda, be there when the kids get home from school, and so on. In other words, it's not even about 'happiness' as such, but having a more relaxed family life, where we have time and freedom to enjoy each other's company, instead of squeezing in quality time around other commitments.

When I asked my Rat Racer friend what happiness looked like to him, he seemed a bit puzzled. He thought for a moment.

'You know, the usual. No stress. Just . . . being happy.'

And this from a guy who worked in sales, and was used to having specific targets each month!

I tried a different approach. 'Alright, if you could be anything or do anything or have anything in the world, what would it be?'

I could almost feel his eye roll.

'Anything at all,' I prompted. 'Go wild. What about an Olympic cyclist?' George had recently discovered the joys of Lycra and weekend cycling.

He gave a tired chuckle. 'At my age?'

'Why not?' I said. 'That American cyclist was older than us when she won gold. But forget about *how*, forget the practicalities and potential obstacles. If you could do anything or be anything or have anything, what would it be?'

George thought for a moment.

THE TRUTH ABOUT MATERIAL GOALS

'Go on then,' he finally said. 'I'll have a Ferrari.'

I had to smile at that. Because what he didn't know is that, once upon a time, I'd wanted the same thing. I desperately wanted a Ferrari in my twenties. (I told you I was a total car nut.) I was deadly serious about it, too. I'd visualise myself driving around town in my Ferrari. I pictured the colour of the paintwork, the feel of the leather seats, the rumble of the engine . . . every bit of it. And when I finally bought myself one, the first time I became a millionaire, I lost everything soon after. Like a messed-up magic trick, the Ferrari disapparated and in its place appeared a £100 Peugeot 106.

I'd since learned not to get too caught up on material goals. Sure, I was still striving for certain material things - I had my monthly passive income goal and that dream house with the woodland in mind. But I wanted those things, not for the *things* themselves, but for how they would benefit me and my family. That dream home was, at its heart, about quality family time and giving my kids a magical childhood. Passive income was about freedom to be my own boss and work when it suits me.

I told George the story of my ill-fated Ferrari and he looked at me with a mixture of envy and disbelief.

'Thing is, George,' I smiled at him. 'When you focus only on the *thing* itself, you may achieve it, but it might not bring you the fulfilment you crave - or, like me and my Ferrari, it just might not turn out the way you expected.'

HOW TO SET GOALS LIKE AN EXTRAORDINARY MILLIONAIRE

The first lesson we can learn from my Rat Racer friend is to set specific, measurable goals - like striving for a particular level of monthly passive income rather than simply 'being rich'. Of course, the level of passive income that I'm striving for now is higher than it was in those early days, as my family has grown and my goals have evolved. It's not like goals have to be unchanging, set in stone. It's natural for goals to shift over time. But they do need to be specific. (Visualisation is a great way to focus on specific outcomes that you want to achieve, but I'll talk more about that in Chapter 2.)

So ask yourself, what do you *really* want out of life? What will bring you joy and satisfaction and those all-important feelings of abundance and freedom?

While it's fine to set material goals, understand *why* you want those material things. Even now, I still set material goals, particularly around my monthly passive income. But it's always focused on the bigger picture of *why* I want that - for instance, so I can have a certain lifestyle with my family and have more time for non-work stuff.

And as I said to George, don't get too hung up on the practicalities of how you'll achieve your goals. The practical action comes later. Don't let fear of failure hold you back either (see Chapter 14), just concentrate on identifying what's most important to you.

When visualising my dream family home, I could easily have gone down a rabbit hole of, 'But I'll need X amount of money up front. And how huge will the mortgage be on a house like that? And there aren't even a lot of properties in this part of the country with their own bit of woodland. How will we find what we want? Would we have to move to a different area? But what about schools?' Weighed down by obstacles and practicalities, it's all too easy to give up and never go after that you want.

The first step, then, is to define what you really want, being as specific as you can, without worrying about the *how*. Instead, think about *why* you want to achieve those goals. What will it mean to your life and your loved ones?

It's even more powerful if you can connect your goals to your passion.

TAPPING INTO PASSION

Flashback to my early twenties, when I was doing an engineering-based degree and I enrolled on an IT summer course – nothing to do with my degree, mind, but I thought it looked interesting. At the time, IT-related careers were starting to boom and frequently listed among the highest-earning jobs in the UK. 'I'll do that for a living,' I thought, purely based on the prospect of earning decent money. But I soon found out that working in IT, while lucrative and secure, just didn't light my fire. I wasn't connecting to my passion.

Incidentally, George had a similar start to his working life. His mother had worked in sales and built a steady, relatively lucrative career. He didn't go into sales because he was passionate about selling B2B technology solutions; it was a means to an end, that's all.

How many times have you heard someone say, 'I still don't know what I want to do with my life?' I hear it a lot. Maybe you've said it yourself. For me, that phrase translates into 'I don't know what I'm passionate about.' And if you haven't found your passion, how can you set a course for what you want?

My passion found me when I began renting out the two spare bedrooms in my then bachelor pad. Suddenly, I was earning a passive income on the side of my regular job and a whole new world of property investing and passive income was revealed to me. I was hooked, and from this small spark grew a set of goals around increasing my passive income, working for myself, building a business, and so on. That was when I left my steady job and began turning my passion into a business.

When defining your goals, the biggest tip I can give you is to connect them to your passion - be it a hobby, an aspirational feeling (independence, for example, or freedom), a place, certain people, or whatever. Those are the kinds of goals that stick.

WOULD YOU LIKE TO SUPERSIZE THAT?

There's a certain school of thought in goal-setting that says you should set outrageously ambitious goals. Want your business to turn over £500k this year? Why not double that instead? Or triple it? Or multiply it by 10?

Want to double your mailing list within the next three months? Why not within the next month?

Just go bigger. Go big or go home. Do more. Do it faster. More, faster, more, faster.

I love an ambitious goal, but every ambitious goal has its costs in terms of time, energy and resources. For example, I recently set a goal for my business to double our output of YouTube videos for the following month. YouTube is a fast-growing area for us, bringing in high-quality leads, so it's a goal that made sense. And we did it. We doubled our YouTube output for the next month. And it was great. But to achieve that goal we had to double our video marketing budget, and double our freelance resources. On balance, it was worth it, but I wouldn't want to double it again for the following month, and again the month after that. Better for my business (and my sanity) to do another big video push in, say, six months' time.

The Extraordinary Millionaire way is to find a balance between striving for success, and being happy and fulfilled. Call it the 'sweet spot' if you will. The perfect needle point on the gauge where you're challenging yourself and working hard towards what you want, but not running yourself into the ground. I can't tell you where that needle point is on your gauge. But don't feel guilty if it's in an entirely different place to everyone else's.

Not sure where your sweet spot is? Try setting an ambitious target in an area that's well within your control – such as growing your LinkedIn network by a set number of contacts a week or increasing your company's social media posts from once a day to twice a day – and doing that for a trial period. How did it make you feel to push yourself in that way? Was it inspiring? Draining? What have you learned about your limits that can help you set better goals in future?

There's another approach to goal-setting that looks at what your competitors are doing, and pushing yourself to be better than them. Stuck in the rat race, my friend next door was a big fan of this approach, always looking to one-up the latest top performer in his sales department.

I don't buy into that approach, myself. If I only focus on being better than a particular competitor, then I may end up a bit better than them, but there's always going to be another competitor around the corner. Personally, I prefer to focus on my own goals and being the best I can be – and, as a bonus, I'm less stressed because I'm not constantly trying to one-up others in my field. Besides, there's plenty of success to go around.

UNDERSTANDING YOUR MOTIVATORS

If you're going to become successful, you've got to know how you operate. You've got to learn what motivates you. What makes you tick. Especially if you want to become an entrepreneur, where you won't have a boss or corporate agenda dictating what you do every day. You have to motivate yourself to set goals and achieve them.

I find the 'push and pull' theories of motivation helpful here. If you're not familiar with push and pull motivators, it's worth learning about them. But, in essence, a push motivator is something that you have to complete in order to satisfy a need. You force yourself to get it done because you *have* to. Like when I was at school and I would leave my homework until the last possible day. I had to do it then because otherwise I'd get in trouble. That's an example of push motivation. Likewise, my Rat Racer friend was staying in his rat race lane, going to work each day when he didn't want to, because he had a mortgage to pay. That was his push motivator.

In contrast, a pull motivator is something that you're drawn to on your own terms. The desire to do that thing comes from deep within you, not an external force. My goal of living in that dream family home with the beautiful woodland was definitely a pull motivator. It made me want to go out and grab it. It inspired me.

Personally, I think it's okay to be motivated by both push and pull factors. I'm a hugely entrepreneurial person, driven to start new businesses and grow my wealth, because I'm excited to do that stuff. The desire, the drive for that comes from within. But, like most people, I can procrastinate and put off certain tasks that don't inspire me. Admin stuff, anything too detailed is generally a turn-off for me, and I need push motivators to get those things done. (I also surround myself with team members who are better suited to those tasks than me, but more on that later in the book.)

Financially, I also like to be pushed sometimes. If my business needs to increase cash flow in order to pull off an important deal, that will drive me to get off my butt and make more money.

In other words, I like to strike a balance between push and pull motivators, because that works for me. That's how I tick. Ask yourself, what makes *you* tick? In other words, when you begin to pin down your goals and connect to your passion, also give some thought to your motivators. Are you pulled towards that goal by something within you or will you benefit from the added oomph of a push motivator?

TIME TO GET A BIT BLUE PETER

Fast-forward in our story to the point where my wife and I have three beautiful children. My property business was thriving again by this time and I was busier than ever. So busy, in fact, that I'd almost lost sight of why I was doing it in the first place. Don't get me wrong, I loved property more than ever - especially the challenge of taking an unloved, unused building and turning it into something that people want to live in. But I'd lost focus on my bigger-picture goals. That dream family home. The zipline in the woods. More quality time as a family. Bonfires and hammocks and all that stuff. I needed to reconnect and recommit to my goals.

It took a craft session with my oldest daughter to remind me.

We've always encouraged our kids to make 'dream boards' - a simple collage of pictures and words that, basically, capture on paper what they want. Committing to what you want on paper is a crucial step in turning a dream into a goal because it concentrates the mind, helps to maintain focus, and serves as a visual reminder of goals. It's fun, too, especially if you go to town on the aspirational pictures.

Sitting with my oldest daughter as she made a new dream board, I was reminded how powerful this technique is. My daughter's previous dream board was like a snapshot of her younger self - a time capsule of the things that mattered most to her when she was a couple of years younger. It included a personal safe to put her toys in away from her little sister, and a diary with a code lock on it - she was heavily into personal privacy at the time, as you can probably tell. There was a picture of a treehouse on there. She also wanted to fly, to win 'scariest dressed' at the Halloween disco, and to have an adult-size bed. And, much to my horror, she wanted a wedding.

Her goals were evolving before my eyes. Among the images and words on the new dream board were exciting places to visit, and a goal of becoming an artist. Her focus was shifting away from the small material things that we all wish for when we're kids (I had a dream board when I was a kid and it was full of toys and sweets and things I'd quickly grow out of) and evolving towards goals that centred more on experiences and personal fulfilment. I was pleased to see the treehouse stayed, though . . .

I pulled up my own version of the dream board, a simple notes document on my phone listing my personal and professional goals, and I was shocked to see how neglected it had become. There were things on there I'd achieved long ago, and things that no longer mattered to me. Together, we spent a happy hour talking about what we wanted to do/be/have, plus the merits of various treehouse designs, and getting those thoughts down on paper - or in my case, capturing a digital list.

And yes, I know, 'dream board' isn't the best name for this tool. It should be called a 'goal board' or something more action-oriented. Feel free to call yours whatever you like. Here, I've just used the more common terminology. Your dream board doesn't even need to be a visual thing - it could just be a simple written list. Right now, my dream board is a list with a number of embedded pictures that I keep in my phone in a note-taking app called Evernote, so I can refer to it when I'm on the move and easily add or update items. The images aren't essential, but I find they help me form a mental picture of my goals - which, again, brings a new level of clarity and certainty.

Whatever format you choose, the important thing is to take your carefully defined goals and commit to them on paper (or on screen). Then, don't just forget about them; refer to your dream board regularly, perhaps even as part of your daily routine. Ideally, then, you'd take your dream board, or whatever it is, and place it somewhere prominent. If it's a digital document, pin it to the home screen of your phone, so you see it every day. With regular use, the dream board focuses your mind and serves as a great visualisation prompt (but more on that in the next chapter).

Inspired by my daughter, I now update my dream board more often. Whenever I achieve one of the goals, I strike it off the list - which is super-satisfying - and whenever I come up with a new goal, big or small, I add it. And sometimes goals just change, so I amend or delete them. They might not be relevant anymore or I might decide something isn't challenging enough. Having a dream board helps you maintain focus, but you don't want to get too rigid with it. So allow yourself the freedom to amend your dream board when appropriate.

AND · · · ACTION!

We've talked a lot about the difference between goals and dreams, but now we get to the biggest difference of all: action. You can have all sorts of ambitious dreams, but if you never do anything about it, that's all they'll ever be. As soon as you start taking action, a dream – however crazy it may be – becomes a goal.

So although the Rat Racer and the Extraordinary Millionaire want similar things, one of us is much more likely to get there. No prizes for guessing which one. The one who takes action.

Remember when I said to not focus on the specifics of *how* you'll achieve your goals, just focus on what you want? This is the part of the journey where you think about the *how*. Having defined your goals and committed them to paper, now's the time to plan how you'll pull it off.

This is the part that a Rat Racer rarely gets to. Even if he does get as far as defining a clear goal, someone with the Rat Racer mindset will simply sit back and wait for it to just . . . happen for them.

Let's say George had set himself a crazy ambitious goal of competing in the Olympics in his thirties. There are certainly steps he could take in that direction, including implementing a strict training and diet regime, hiring a trainer, putting in dozens of hours of work each week, competing in local competitions, and so on. It's a wild example, I know, but even if he didn't make it to the Olympics, he'd be a damn sight better at cycling than he was at the start. His action would have led him to make huge improvements, achieve personal satisfaction, and maybe even to define some new goals, like winning local races or even tackling a long-distance race.

Even as a kid, I always wanted to have my own business. I was in love with the creative side of being an entrepreneur – creating something (a product or service) that didn't exist before and somehow convincing people that they needed to buy it. I started my first business when I was still in primary school. Alright, it was only selling sherbet to my friends, but it still required some planning. I took my dream of being an entrepreneur and broke it down into actionable chunks. First I had to invest my pocket money in buying various different sherbets from a local sweet shop, then I had to buy little food bags to put my rebranded sherbet in. Next, I came up with interesting flavour combinations that would delight my sweet-toothed friends, then I mixed the various sherbets together and bagged them up. Only then could I take my carefully packaged goodies into school and start selling. It wasn't long before customers were coming to me - friends and neighbours would come to my house to get their hands on my famous sherbet concoctions.

It was a small start, but it taught me that when you take action, you can achieve pretty much anything. So when my youngest daughter told me that she wanted to be a YouTuber when she grew up, I told her of course she could - she could be anything she wanted to be. We talked about what steps she might need take in future to bring that dream to life. We talked about how she'd need a hook - something that makes her stand out in a world where (in my experience, at least) 90% of her friends also want to be YouTubers! And we talked about how she could use YouTube as a tool to grow a career that she's truly passionate about - as opposed to just unboxing products for random internet strangers to watch.

What about deadlines? Should you assign a timetable to your goals? Many people say not to put a time limit on your goals and, for the most part, I agree. However, some of my goals will have a natural timetable of their own, such as those related to my business. And, of course, I wanted that dream home with the woodland while my kids were still young enough to enjoy it. So I say set a target date where appropriate, and only if it helps you, but don't get too hung up on a timetable for everything. You don't want to suck the joy out of setting goals.

URGENT VS IMPORTANT

When I had my dream-board epiphany, helping my daughter update her dream board and realising how neglected mine was, I had another realisation. I realised part of the reason I had been neglecting my goals was because I was too busy firefighting the urgent stuff every day and neglecting the *important* stuff.

And there is a difference between the two. As President Eisenhower put it, 'What is important is seldom urgent and what is urgent is seldom important.' The urgent tasks are the ones that scream for your attention right now, but aren't necessarily that critical in the grand scheme of achieving your goals. Meanwhile, the important tasks are those that will take you closer to whatever it is you really want.

Take emails as an example. I was spending hours and hours every day dealing with my emails, when most of them weren't mission-critical in terms of growing my business, generating new leads, growing my income, and so on. Meanwhile, I was struggling to prioritise the strategically important tasks, like finally finishing the book I was working on at the time, or seeking out new freelancers to help manage my workload.

My Rat Racer neighbour knew exactly what I was on about. His problem was meetings. Endless meetings at work that sucked his time and energy away from more important tasks.

'It's just the way it is though, isn't it?' he lamented. 'Until I learn to clone myself or someone invents a 30-hour day.'

I can't magically make more hours in the day – if I could I'd have done it years ago. But I can tell you to make sure you prioritise the important stuff. Every day.

Some people find it helpful to set a daily to-do list, with the items listed in order of priority – the idea being you don't move onto a less-important task until you've done the most important stuff first. Me? I needed heavier reinforcements. I needed someone to hold me accountable.

WHO'S HOLDING YOU ACCOUNTABLE?

When I told George I'd hired an accountability coach, he couldn't believe his ears. He couldn't believe I'd hired someone to, as he described it, 'nag me for a living'.

But my accountability coach does much more than that. They help me set goals, prioritise action steps to achieve those goals and, yes, they basically chase me up until I do it. As a description, 'professional nag' isn't that far off the mark. But for me, it works. That said, I appreciate it's not everyone's cup of tea. Nor does everyone need that level of reinforcement.

If you're the type of person who can set a goal and hold yourself accountable day in day out, until you meet your goal, I applaud you. Personally, I need a little extra help in that department. I need others to help me stay focused on my goals. And I'm not just talking about hiring an accountability coach (although I will say it's been brilliant); I'm talking about sharing my goals with friends and family, and asking them to help keep me honest.

It's the reason why people go to weight-loss groups and endure weekly weigh-ins. Because they know it keeps them accountable. They know it helps them stay focused, stick to their weight loss journey, and achieve their target weight. And what happens when they stop going to the group - whether they've met their target weight or not? They're no longer accountable and, for many dieters, at least, they end up falling hard off the wagon.

It's the same with other goals. You need a mechanism to keep you accountable. For me, telling family and friends (including my Rat Racer friend), 'I'm going to do X, Y and Z' makes me much more likely to achieve those goals. And it's even better when my family and I set joint goals together, and commit to achieving them, together.

Like making mornings less chaotic - something my wife and I, and our kids, all really wanted to do. The kids wanted us to stop hassling them every five minutes in the morning, and my wife and I just wanted to get out the door on time. So we devised a game where the first person to be fully ready - and I mean fully ready, shoes on, school bag packed, not forgetting anything - and out to the car on time is the winner for the day. (If, like me, you have competitive kids, it's a good way to make mornings less stressful.)

In other words, don't underestimate the boost others can give to your goals. They can help you stay focused on what you want, cheerlead you when you flag, and give you a kick up the backside when your actions don't support your goals.

GOAL-SETTING LESSONS FROM THE RAT RACER AND THE EXTRAORDINARY MILLIONAIRE

- The Rat Racer doesn't think too hard about what they really want from life. When they do think about it, they'll plump for general wishes like being 'rich' and 'happy' and 'successful'.
- In contrast, the Extraordinary Millionaire defines exactly what they want and why. Their goals tie into their passions.
- The Rat Racer gets immediately bogged down in *how* they'll achieve something (or, more likely, why they can't achieve it).
- The Extraordinary Millionaire begins by focusing only on what they want. They'll work out the specific actions later.
- The Rat Racer avoids putting themselves out there and publicly committing to their goals.
- The Extraordinary Millionaire knows that committing to their goals verbally and on paper - using a dream board or similar tool - is vital.
- The Rat Racer sits back and waits for what they want to come to them.
- The Extraordinary Millionaire identifies the steps required to achieve their goal, and tackles it one step at a time - keeping a laser-like focus on what's important, rather than being permanently distracted by urgent firefighting tasks. They hold themselves accountable, and they ask others to help keep them accountable along the way.

As I got better at defining and focusing on my goals, something interesting began to happen. I was automatically beginning to hold my goals in my heart and my thoughts, without needing to manually prompt myself (for example, by looking at my dream board). My goals were with me, all the time, and I was forming clear mental pictures of these goals, constantly visualising them and working to manifest them, without even consciously noticing that's what I was doing. It took the realisation of a seriously big, hairy goal for me to notice how hard I was holding this mental picture in my head. It was a true lightbulb moment – I'd discovered the incredible power of our next Extraordinary Millionaire technique: visualisation.

Chapter 2

Using Visualisation to Bring Your Goals to Life

'All you need now is your own TV show,' said the neighbour, George.

We were having one of those 'how's work going?' conversations as we passed each other in the front garden. The kind of conversation we'd had a hundred times. But this time was different. Because my Rat Racer friend's throwaway joke - that everything else was going so well in my business, the only thing missing was my own property show - sparked a recognition in me. It surfaced a goal that I'd been subconsciously harbouring for a while.

By this point, I'd started mentoring aspiring property developers, helping them realise their property goals - while growing my own property portfolio - and I'd discovered a passion for educating others. I was also putting out educational YouTube videos and starting to publish ebooks by this point. But what better way to educate a wider audience than with a TV programme aimed at property investors?

'You're right,' I agreed. 'I do need a TV show. That's what I'll do.'

My Rat Racer friend laughed and shook his head, 'I bet you will as well.'

We were both at good places in our lives. He had recently been promoted and was now responsible for a bigger sales region. His family was growing, as was mine, and our young kids were always in and out of each other's houses. Our friendship had grown. As such, I knew that he was also harbouring a big dream. He had an idea for a cycling-related app - the cycling equivalent of that popular 'Couch to 5 kilometres' running app - that he wanted to turn into a business. He wanted out of the rat race. To be his own boss.

Although he talked about it often, it was still just a dream. He hadn't taken any action towards it yet, not even baby steps. With two young kids and a mortgage to pay, quitting his well-paid job seemed nuts to him. And the very idea of getting his app off the ground as a side-hustle, while working full time and raising a family, was exhausting.

It became a gentle running joke between us.

'Haven't seen you on TV yet,' he'd rib me.

'How's the app coming?' I'd respond.

I didn't mind his poking fun at me, because I had an unshakable confidence that I would get my TV show and grow my reputation as an expert property investor. I was visualising it. Just as I was visualising my other goals - including that dream family home with the woodland and zip line. By visualising the things I wanted, picturing them with astonishing clarity and detail, I was breathing life into my goals on a daily basis. And with that, came a calming sense of certainty. It may sound weird, but the simple act of visualising my goals made me believe with even more confidence that I would achieve them. I could *see* it happening. I could *feel* it.

ISN'T VISUALISATION JUST DAYDREAMING?

That was George's question when I mentioned visualisation (or 'creative visualisation' as it's often called).

'So, what, you're basically daydreaming?' he asked.

'In a sense, yes,' I answered. 'Visualisation is just grown-up daydreaming - something that we all indulge in from time to me, whether you daydream about being on a tropical beach as you sit in a rainy traffic jam, or imagine yourself rocking out on the Pyramid Stage at Glastonbury! Visualisation means taking that ability to daydream and applying it in a more focused, structured way that gets you closer to your goals.'

'But how does it get you closer to your goals?' he asked.

'I know from experience that when I visualise what I want on a regular basis, I begin to live and act with those goals in mind. I say yes to opportunities that I might otherwise have shied away from. I feel calmer and more positive. I have a greater feeling of purpose. I'm more focused on my goals, basically. They're constantly with me, in my heart and my mind, because I can picture them with such clarity. Does that make sense?'

George thought for a moment. 'Well, I can certainly see the appeal of daydreaming about things you want. But does it really have an impact on success? *That* I'm not so sure about.'

'Let me put it this way,' I countered. 'Visualisation is mentioned as far back as Napoleon Hill's wildly successful *Think and Grow Rich*. And that was published in the 1930s. So we're talking about a long history of visualisation being used as a business and self-help tool. It's also used a lot in sports. Golfer Jack Nicklaus once said his success was 10% technique, 40% set-up, and 50% visualisation.'

VISUALISING THE BIG STUFF, AND THE SMALL STUFF

George gave a wry smile. 'So what you're telling me is I should just daydream about being a tech billionaire lounging on my yacht in Monte Carlo?'

'You could . . .' I said. 'But if I were you I'd visualise the outcomes I want, rather than just possessions or having a big pile of money.'

'Maybe the outcome I really want is a yacht. A big one, with a helicopter on top.' His knowing smile said he was joking with me. He clearly thought my visualisation habit was verging on the woo-woo.

'Okay, fine.' I played along. 'In that case, you could visualise yourself stepping onto your yacht for the first time. Feeling the sunshine on your face as you hand your luggage over to one of your crew. The smell of the salty air and the sound of seagulls as you're handed a cold glass of–'

'No seagulls,' he interrupted me. 'If this is my fantasy, I don't want any seagulls dropping their load on my brand new yacht.'

'You're missing the point,' I laughed.

'Which is?'

'What you really want isn't the yacht at all. What you really want is to be a successful tech entrepreneur, working for yourself, setting your own agenda, working when you want and having the time and freedom - and, yes, the money - to pop off to Monaco if the mood strikes you.'

'I'm listening . . .' he said.

'The boat's just a distraction. I mean, you can visualise it if you want to. I'll sometimes visualise myself riding down Route 66 on a beautiful red Harley Davidson. It's a bit of fun. But I prefer to spend my energy imagining more meaningful outcomes.'

'Like presenting your own property TV programme?'

'Yeah. Or watching my kids run around the woodland at our future dream family home. You know, having a certain freedom and lifestyle. But those scenarios can be anything you want, and they don't even have to be big, hairy goals. You can visualise small outcomes and achievements, as well.'

'Like a perfect family holiday, or something like that?' George asked.

'Or even smaller and more immediate than that. Like giving an awesome presentation tomorrow, or impressing a new client at your first meeting. In fact, my wife and I get the kids to visualise stuff they're nervous about, so they can picture it going well.'

'Oh yeah?'

'Case in point, last week my daughter was nervous about her role in the school play. She'd been rehearsing her short speech all week and had it memorised beautifully, but her nerves were getting the better of her. She was so worried about forgetting her lines or saying the wrong thing. Or worse, everyone laughing at her. So I gave her the same advice I'd give myself if I were getting up on stage in front of people.'

'Which is . . .' George prompted.

'I told her to picture herself speaking her lines perfectly and having fun up on the stage. I encouraged her to imagine the audience clapping loudly at the end. To imagine how great she would feel afterwards, her and her friends, knowing that they did an awesome job together. To just imagine herself nailing it, basically, and focus on how good that feels.

I told her to keep picturing that, over and over again, right up until the moment when she went on stage.'

'And how did it go?' he asked.

I smiled at the memory of the school play, seeing my daughter embrace the experience. 'Well, like any school play, there were one or two cute mishaps, but it went down a storm. And more importantly, she was able to overcome her nerves and have fun with her friends. Seriously, this stuff isn't just for adults. It's a great way for kids to boost their confidence and ease anxiety. If you ask me, visualisation should be taught in schools to help young people plan for success in their lives. This is exactly the sort of skill we should be passing on to the next generation.'

George nodded. 'Lily is freaking out about her upcoming SATs tests. Maybe this could give her a boost?'

'I bet it would. We regularly use visualisation with the kids. And you know what? They find it fun, because they can let their imagination loose. Give it a try.'

In this way, visualisation isn't just about helping you achieve your goals (although it's fantastic for that). It's a really useful technique to pull out of the bag when negative thoughts or doubt creep in - and that goes for whether you're nervous about giving a presentation, scared of flying, or simply trying to help your kids grow in confidence.

Let's see how you can use visualisation to achieve your goals, big and small, and to boost your positivity in general.

WHAT DO YOU WANT TO VISUALISE?

Visualisation is at its most powerful when you focus on specific goals or outcomes, rather than material possessions or general wishes like 'I want to be successful'. Which is why this technique follows on from goal-setting. First you need to define exactly what you want, then you can use visualisation as a tool to help bring those goals to life, ideally by imagining super-specific scenarios.

But those scenarios can be anything you want. In fact, what I love about visualisation is it can be used to breathe life into literally any kind of goal. Take our dream family home as an example. I visualised scenarios like holding the keys in my hand and opening the front door for the first time, then watching my kids run upstairs and argue over who gets which room. I pictured my wife and I in the garden, enjoying a glass of wine in the sunshine as our kids ran wild in the woodland. I pictured us erecting a zip line, just as I'd done in my childhood. I pictured myself working in a garden office overlooking nothing but trees and greenery . . .

To aid this process of visualisation, my wife and I would do things like looking at dream houses on Rightmove and driving by beautiful houses in areas we admired. Sometimes, we even viewed houses which, at that point, were beyond our means. For us, it was all part of our goal-setting, manifestation and visualisation process, just like having a dream board. In fact, we found that looking at houses in real life (either from the curb or on actual viewings) was even more powerful than just having a picture of a beautiful house on a dream board.

But back to you. What outcomes are you seeking? Want to start your own business? Then visualise yourself in your brand-new office or shaking hands with your first investor. Want to grow your wealth and achieve financial independence? Visualise yourself handing in your notice at your job, having built a steady passive income stream. Want to find a loving relationship? Visualise yourself on a Sunday morning stroll, holding hands with your loved one as you walk your dog together.

When author Gabrielle Bernstein was writing her first book, she didn't have a publisher lined up. But she held visions in her head of herself as an author. She also visualised herself as a speaker and teacher, speaking on the same stages as her heroes, people like the late author and motivational speaker Dr Wayne Dyer. Gabrielle signed her first book deal in 2009. A few years later, after publishing three more books, she gave a talk to a huge audience at the Javits Center in New York, standing in the exact spot where her hero Wayne Dyer had given a speech years before (while Gabrielle sat watching from the front row). Her long-held vision had come true. She is now a New York Times bestselling author and international speaker.

Bottom line, whatever big life changes you're after, visualisation can help you get there. But it works best when you focus on a specific goal or set of goals.

Those goals can be as big and hairy as you like, like me picturing myself presenting a TV programme for property investors. In fact, I find big, crazy daydreams to be inspiring. What's the point of only visualising in half measures? But as my daughter's school play shows, visualisation can also be used to achieve much smaller goals and flip negative thoughts into positive ones.

I use visualisation techniques all the time to picture small things that I want to go well, like an important meeting. Just a few minutes visualising how I want the meeting to go delivers dramatic results. I find I perform far better in a meeting that I've visualised in advance, because I've fully thought through various scenarios, planned for a successful outcome, and generally given my confidence a boost.

In a way, then, visualisation is a tool for planning things you didn't realise you could plan for, such as making a great first impression when you meet someone for the first time, performing well in a job interview, or even cooking a celebratory meal to perfection. Visualisation can help you prepare for any kind of situation or event - work or otherwise - and plan for it to go well. By visualising a positive outcome, I find it easier to tap into feelings of positivity and calm - and I perform better as a result because I'm less stressed and more confident in my abilities. Visualisation is therefore an excellent technique to use in any kind of high-stress or high-stakes situation.

People often rely on things like diaries, to-do lists and calendar reminders as planning tools, and those certainly have their place. But all those tools really do is help you plan your *time.* They don't help you plan your performance or specific outcomes. Visualisation is a really powerful way to plan for performance and outcomes. That's why I like to think of it as another tool in my planning toolkit, along with things like reminders, notifications and diaries.

Visualisation can also help you change your behaviour, embrace new skills, and even build new habits. I'm not a particularly confident public speaker - a significant obstacle for someone who visualises themselves presenting on TV! So I also use visualisation to help me reprogramme my mind, so that I start to think and act like someone who is a confident presenter. (It's easy to see why visualisation often forms a part of other success-building practices, like neuro-linguistic programming.)

If you also get nervous speaking in front of a crowd, try doing what I do and imagine yourself delivering an engaging speech to a rapt audience and *enjoying yourself* in the process. (The enjoying yourself part is key, but we'll talk more about tapping into emotions later.) Keep doing that exercise and, over time, you'll start to think of yourself as a confident, enthusiastic public speaker.

TRUST ME, I'M A DOCTOR - THE VERY REAL BENEFITS OF VISUALISATION

Okay, I'm not a doctor, but I do know that medical studies have found visualisation speeds recovery, helping patients recover from surgery faster than those patients who don't use visualisation techniques. It has also been proven to help athletes recover from injury faster.

Why would this be the case? Why would daydreaming - which is, after all, basically what visualisation is - have proven physical effects? Probably for the same reason I find visualisation to be so potent. Because it lowers stress (which has been shown to hinder healing), and enhances feelings of calmness and positivity.

Have you ever had a raging hangover, or felt a cold coming on, and found yourself focusing on how awful you felt? The more you think about how bad you feel, or how you can't afford to get sick right now, the worse you feel. Positive visualisation is the flip side of that coin. When you imagine yourself in excellent health, feeling well and full of energy, it reprogrammes the mind, and the body responds accordingly. You might not fully stave off that cold, but you'll be less likely to collapse in a sad heap on the sofa.

Speaking from experience, I've found visualisation also helps to enhance my concentration. Whether I'm picturing a big life goal or a small scenario like a successful presentation, I feel more focused after a brief visualisation exercise.

Part of the reason why visualisation is so powerful is that it's basically a form of creative thinking. And creative thinking is an important predictor of success (both academic success and life success). In fact, some experts believe creativity is a bigger predictor of success than intelligence. How cool is that? By tapping into our imagination, we're sowing the seeds for success. If you were ever the kind of child that was told by teachers to 'stop daydreaming', you can finally feel vindicated. Because our ability to daydream, to imagine exciting new possibilities, is a big part of what makes us human, and has allowed the human race to come so far. It's bizarre to think that daydreaming is ever considered a negative trait or a waste of time, when the reality is it's a powerful force for good.

Of course, it's only a powerful force for good if you use visualisation to imagine positive scenarios and outcomes. It can be all too easy to slip into imagining negative scenarios or all the things that *might* go wrong, like fluffing your lines in the school play, or being on a plane and it crashing into the sea. Which brings us onto some practical visualisation tips . . .

THE RIGHT WAY TO VISUALISE

First up, let me reiterate the importance of setting clear goals. Rather than focusing on general wishes, visualisation works best when applied to more concrete desired outcomes. For example, instead of simply wanting to be healthy, visualise yourself running five times a week, building up to a high level of fitness and feeling fantastic as a result. Or, instead of just wanting to be a famous writer, imagine yourself opening a parcel from your publisher and seeing your debut book inside. Imagine holding your beautiful book in your hand and smelling that 'new book' smell as you flip through its pages.

For those big life goals, it helps to commit to your goals on paper, either using a dream board, like my daughter and I did in Chapter 1, or by making a simple bullet list of goals. This concentrates the mind on what you really want, and serves as a useful prompt when you sit down to visualise. You can visualise one, two or all of the things on your dream board, depending on how long your list of goals is and how much time you have that day.

If you want to visualise a smaller scenario, like performing well in a meeting or making a great impression on a first date, just spend a few minutes getting clear on your desired outcome before you sit down to visualise. Remember, visualisation is a focused, structured form of daydreaming - you're not just letting your mind wander off wherever it wants.

Ready to daydream? Here's an example of how I sit down and visualise one of my goals:

I get comfy on the sofa in my home office. It's early morning and the kids are stirring, but the house hasn't yet reached that manic morning phase. Everything is still peaceful.

I pull up my list of goals on my phone. There are several on there, but today I want to focus on just one goal: presenting a property investment TV show.

I close my eyes and form a clear mental image of me accomplishing that goal. In the image, I'm in a studio. There's a director and a couple of camera operators. I'm talking to the camera about what makes a great investment property. I'm speaking articulately and with confidence. All my preparation has paid off.

The director shouts 'Cut!' She tells me, 'Nice one, Nicholas. That's all for today.' I've finished my first ever day of filming.

The image is so vivid and rich. I can see what I'm wearing, right down to the little microphone pinned to my shirt. I can feel the warmth of the studio lights on me. I can smell the freshly brewed coffee, waiting for us now that we've finished filming.

I tap into the emotions I feel having accomplished this huge goal. I feel proud. I can't wait to call my wife and tell her how it went. I'm excited for the next day of filming, and for people to watch the show. I feel grateful for this opportunity. I feel elated. I'm smiling in my vision, and in real life, as the emotions wash over me. I feel overcome, almost on the verge of tears, the sensation of joy is so strong.

Finally, I let a feeling of certainty settle over me. Certainty that I will one day realise this vision. It will all come to fruition. It's intensely reassuring.

I sit in silence for a few minutes, holding this vivid picture in my mind and enjoying the sensations that go with it.

Try following this basic pattern yourself:

- Create a vivid and rich mental image of achieving the thing you want.
- Tap into the positive feelings that go along with achieving that goal (big or small).
- Settle into a feeling of certainty.

That last point is crucial. The biggest piece of visualisation advice I can give you is to *believe*. Believe in what you're visualising. You need to believe it can, and will, happen. You need to believe your visualisation is the absolutely true version of your future. If you don't, the whole process is undermined. As Gabrielle Bernstein puts it, 'Certainty of outcome is the secret ingredient.'

Most of us have a lot of responsibilities in life and, sometimes, aiming for ambitious new goals can feel like we're heaping yet more pressure on top. But the beauty of visualisation is that, used properly, it helps attach a sense of calm certainty to your goals. When you visualise yourself achieving everything you want, when you really feel all those feelings of joy and gratitude associated with achieving your goals, it's easy to be certain of your own success. And that's an amazing feeling. Which is why I consider visualisation to be as much of a mental health tool as it is a success-boosting tool.

Give it a try, and I bet you'll be surprised at the powerful feelings that are unleashed by visualisation. I'm not the only one to experience intense positive emotions while visualising. And those positive feelings stay with me, long after I've got up off my office sofa and started making the kids' breakfasts. It's a great way to start the day.

That said, you don't have to visualise in the morning. It can be something you check in with at several times throughout the day - just before going into a meeting, while you're on the train coming home from work, just before you drift off to sleep, or whenever. But I will say that regular practice is key. As with all of the mindset techniques in this book, to get the most out of visualisation, you need to do it often. Ideally daily, but a few times a week is better than nothing. This isn't always easy in the context of a busy life with lots of daily demands, but it's really important to make time for visualisation. (See Chapter 8 for more on building a daily routine.) If you feel too busy or stressed, that's all the more reason to visualise and focus your mind on positive outcomes.

And finally, visualisation is a great way to get you in the right frame of mind for success, but it's not a substitute for taking action. In other words, you can't visualise yourself as an amazing public speaker, and then neglect to prepare for your actual presentation. Action is key. Visualisation will help you breathe life into your goals, boost your self-belief, and create a sense of certainty that you *can and will* do it, but you must also take practical steps and stay open to opportunities that will help you deliver your goals.

HOW *NOT* TO VISUALISE

Visualisation is about filling your brain with images of a bright future - picturing everything that can and will go right. This is in stark contrast to how many of us think. So many of us are plagued by thoughts of what *could* go wrong, or what has gone wrong in the past. So many of us obsess over what we *don't* want to happen, instead of focusing on what we do want.

My Rat Racer friend next door was stuck in this cycle. He desperately wanted out of the rat race, but when he thought of turning his app idea into a business, his mind went straight to the obstacles in his way and everything that might go wrong: not being able to pay his mortgage, ending up broke, being more stressed, feeling uncertain all the time . . .

It's a lesson in how not to visualise. Because, as the law of attraction states, we get what we think about most. So if you fill your head with everything you *don't* want, you're less likely to achieve the things you *do* want. But more on that in the next chapter.

Visualising the positives instead of the negatives doesn't always come naturally. I've had those moments where my brain automatically goes straight for the worst possible outcome. But thoughts can always be changed. You can, quite simply, just decide to think differently.

NEXT-LEVEL VISUALISATION

As with anything, the more you use visualisation, the easier it becomes and the better you get at it. You will, over time, become more focused on your goals. It'll become easier and easier to tap into your visualisation scenarios, whatever they may be, and quickly feel those associated emotions and belief. At that point, visualisation becomes something you can turn to in quiet moments throughout the day, whenever you need a quick burst of positivity or an injection of confidence. In other words, it doesn't always have to be a formal, 'Right, for the next five minutes, I'm going to sit here and VISUALISE' kind of thing. It can be something you do just for a few seconds at a time and still feel the benefits.

Eventually, visualisation becomes an ingrained habit, something you do automatically without consciously thinking about it. Or at least, it has for me and my family. We love our dream boards and goal lists in our household, but I've found that I now hold my goals in my heart and head constantly - I can recall them without needing to look at my dream board quite so often. To put it another way, thanks to visualisation, I'm constantly connected to my goals. They've become mental pictures in my head. They're much more vivid and tangible to me than just words on a piece of paper or a phone screen.

As I write this chapter, I've just started filming The Property Mentors TV show (www.propertymentors.tv) with Homes Under The Hammer presenter Martin Roberts. My crazy goal is coming to life, just as I had pictured it for years. I had one of those 'bolt of lightning' moments when I realised that my goals weren't just words on a piece of paper - they had become vivid mental pictures that were with me all the time, and now those pictures were becoming reality.

And when the director said, 'Cut!' you'd better believe I felt all those same emotions I'd felt, visualising the scene on my office sofa.

VISUALISATION LESSONS FROM THE RAT RACER AND THE EXTRAORDINARY MILLIONAIRE

- The Rat Racer is taught to believe that daydreaming is a waste of time.
- The Extraordinary Millionaire knows that visualisation is a structured form of daydreaming with proven benefits for the mind and body. They know that creative thinking is a key predictor of success.
- If they do indulge in a little daydreaming, the Rat Racer will dream of general wishes, like being filthy rich, rather than specific scenarios.
- The Extraordinary Millionaire uses visualisation to imagine specific outcomes and bring goals - big and small - to life. They also use visualisation to boost confidence, reinforce positive thinking and build helpful habits.
- When thinking about their goals, the Rat Racer pictures everything that might go wrong. They feel all the negative emotions - fear, worry, uncertainty - that go along with failure, even though it hasn't even happened.
- The Extraordinary Millionaire visualises a successful outcome, tapping into all the positive emotions that go along with achieving their goals. They feel joy, pride and gratitude. Most importantly, they

feel a sense of certainty, that they will absolutely achieve the things they want.

- The Rat Racer is too busy for visualisation.
- The Extraordinary Millionaire makes time for a regular visualisation practice, even if it's just a few seconds or minutes at a time. Because they know that visualisation helps them feel calmer, more positive and more focused on their goals.

Visualisation wires the brain for success and creates the conditions in which you can manifest that success - because, by visualising what you want with clarity and certainty, you begin to live with those goals in mind. Just as the law of attraction teaches us. Which brings us onto the next mindset technique in the Extraordinary Millionaire's toolkit . . .

Chapter 3

The Law of Attraction and Living in Abundance

'God, I remember this book. Everyone was reading it back in the day. What's it doing here? Load of mystical nonsense, isn't it?'

My Rat Racer friend George was glancing over my bookshelf and had landed on the enormously popular bestseller, *The Secret*.

'You mean you haven't read it?' I asked.

'Should I?'

'Mate, this book changed my life.'

It was no exaggeration. The simple idea behind this book – the idea that *like attracts like* – perfectly distilled something I'd known deep down for years: that being positive brings more good things your way and being negative attracts more negative stuff. *The Secret* gave me a method to put this super-simple idea into practice. It shaped my actions as I grew my business and worked towards my goals. It still shapes my actions to this day.

George was sceptical. I got where he was coming from. The very phrase 'law of attraction' does have a whiff of New Age woo-woo about it. But scratch the surface and you quickly discover an incredibly practical tool.

So I told him the story of the first time I made the law of attraction work for me.

'I was at probably the lowest point in my life, living in a terrible rental flat in Dover. Absolutely flat broke. Struggling to attract the sort of investors I needed to really get my business off the ground. It was depressing. My mental health was taking a battering. Then I read this book and it helped lift me out of my mental funk. It reminded me that I should be focusing on what I want out of life, and the things that I have, instead of dwelling on everything that's gone wrong and all the things I don't have. At the time, there was this car on my dream board that I wanted–'

George screwed up his face. 'On your what?'

'On my list of goals. One of my goals was to have a Nissan GTR supercar.'

Fellow car nut that he was, George nodded in approval.

I continued, 'I'd wanted one of those for as long as I could remember. And when I read *The Secret* I decided to see if I could manifest it. You know, achieve this goal of owning this gorgeous car, even though I was a broke young guy living in a crappy flat in Dover.'

'And did you?'

I pulled up an old picture of me on my phone. In the photo, I'm standing by my Nissan GTR and looking pretty damn pleased with life.

George nodded in appreciation at the car, but was still sceptical. 'But how did this book,' he waved *The Secret* at me, 'get you that car?'

'Let me explain,' I said.

LIKE ATTRACTS LIKE

'The fundamental principle behind the law of attraction is like attracts like,' I continued. 'It basically means that things - both good and bad - are attracted to us by our thoughts and our feelings. You get back what you put out there, in other words.'

Most of us recognise this phenomenon of getting back what you put out - indeed, most of us have experienced it in everyday situations.

George looked unconvinced, so I asked him, 'Have you ever had one of those days where you feel on top of the world for no particular reason? You just wake up in a great mood and the day gets better and better from there. You put out nothing but positive vibes as you move through your day, you get that positivity reflected back at you. People seem extra-smiley to you. The birds seem to be singing louder than normal. Even your lunchtime sandwich tastes amazing. You get days like that?'

'Of course,' George nodded.

'Contrast that with a day where you wake up on the wrong side of the bed. You snap at your kids in the kitchen. You frown at the barista at the coffee shop as she manages a long list of orders. You show your frustrations with colleagues at the office. And what do you get back in return?'

'More of the same, I guess.' George agreed. 'People snapping back. My mood gets worse. That sort of thing.'

'Exactly!' I said. 'Because like attracts like.'

George isn't alone in having those days. Most of us can relate to being stuck in a cycle of negativity - however brief (or not) it may be. It happens because, as you focus on something, the law of attraction delivers more *like* thoughts and experiences to you. Like attracts like. You snap at others and they snap back at you. You feel impatient and hurried, and more delays and frustrations are attracted your way.

I gave George an example of getting myself stuck in a cycle of negativity.

'A few years ago, I had a problem with one of my property developments being delayed because of planning issues. It dragged on for far longer than I would have liked, and in turn, it was dragging me down. I was irritated. It felt like my normally positive attitude was being chipped away, bit by bit, one frustrating day at a time. This began to show in my attitude at work. Across all my development projects you know I have a lot of people working for me, and I always try to model the right behaviour around my team - to act the way I want others to act and treat others the way I want to be treated myself. But, as my negativity around this project began to push its way to the surface, a culture of negative comments grew around the office. In just a short space of time, morale started to dip. I had forgotten that like attracts like.'

It's easy to fall into a negative cycle, but you can break the cycle by consciously thinking positive thoughts or distracting yourself with a mood-boosting activity. You can choose to feel better, basically. I had to remember that myself.

'So what did you do?' George asked. 'How did you turn it around?'

'I made a conscious effort to show up with a positive attitude and demonstrate the behaviour I wanted to see. As I changed my behaviour, I noticed an almost immediate adjustment in those around me. I projected a positive attitude, which made me *feel* even happier, and, unsurprisingly, this manifested as a dramatic change in those I work with. That challenging project? It was successfully resolved and, in the end, it turned out to be a really profitable development. More importantly, it was a profound learning experience for me.'

'It's interesting to hear you talk like that,' George said. 'You always come off as this super-positive guy. It's quite reassuring, actually, to know you're prone to the odd negative cycle.'

To be clear, I'm not saying that positive people only ever experience happy thoughts and wonderful things in life, while pessimists only ever have bad days. Of course that's not true. Optimists experience low points, ill health, grief, relationship breakups, work frustrations, redundancy, and all the other obstacles that life throws at us. But they move forward, choosing to focus on the good rather than the bad. They give thanks for what they have, rather than focus on what they lack.

'I may lean more towards optimism than pessimism,' I said to George. 'But I make a choice to focus on the positive, rather than the negative. Even when things aren't going to plan. It's like Abraham Lincoln said, "Most folks are as happy as they make up their minds to be."'

George cracked a smile. 'Well, that's just common sense, though.'

'It *is* common sense,' I agreed. 'But that doesn't make the law of attraction any less powerful. What's really amazing is that the law of attraction goes way beyond thoughts, attitude and behaviour. It's also about manifesting the things you most want out of life, whether it's a new job, meeting the love of your life, wealth and abundance, better health, or any other desire. By training the mind to focus on the things you want, you can bring those things into reality. Like I did with that car.'

'But *how* does it work?' George asked.

MANIFESTING WHAT YOU WANT INSTEAD OF WHAT YOU DON'T WANT

'Think of yourself as a magnet,' I said to George. 'Your thoughts give off this magnetic force that attracts the things you think about most. Just like a magnet does. So when people focus on what they *don't* want

- debt, money worries, stress - it stands to reason those things will keep showing up.'

'So you're saying the reason I have a great big load on my credit card is because I'm bringing it on myself, with my thoughts?' he seemed offended.

'Well, I wouldn't put it quite like that,' I said. 'Let's put it this way, the law of attraction says that to attract wealth, you should think about money and wealth and abundance. Not debt. If you think about debt all the time - even if you're thinking "Oh, I wish I could get out of this debt" - you're likely to bring more debt into your life because that's where you put your focus.'

According to the law of attraction, you attract the things you think about the most, good or bad. So when you hear stories of people - myself included - who have attracted a lot of wealth, then lost it all, then made it all back and more (the classic tale of boom, bust, then more boom), that can be explained by the law of attraction. Such people become wealthy because they focus their thoughts on wealth, as opposed to how much money they *don't* have. Then, when they become wealthy, they worry about losing it all. Sure enough, that happens. Then, with their thoughts tuned back to wealth, they prosper again.

'Take your dream of being your own boss,' I said to George. 'You want to get out of the rat race. Get away from the 9 to 5 grind, right?'

'Right,' my Rat Racer friend agreed.

'So what do you think about when you think about that goal? Are you thinking, "God, I don't want to do this job anymore?" or something like that?'

'I guess. Something like that . . .'

'The law of attraction doesn't hear the word "don't". It doesn't understand the *context* of your thoughts, good or bad. It only responds to the *content* of your thoughts, and gives you more of that stuff. In this case, the rat race.'

'So I should be thinking about what exactly?'

'The things you actually want,' I said. 'Freedom, independence, being your own boss, prosperity. When I wanted that Nissan GTR, I didn't tune my thoughts to *not* having that car, or not even having the money for such a car. I thought only of having that car. I visualised it clearly. I imagined myself driving around in it, turning up to investor meetings looking and feeling like a successful person.'

'I still don't really get *how* it works,' my Rat Racer friend said. 'You wanted this car and you eventually managed to afford it. It's not like the universe just gave it to you because you thought about it often enough. You're not a magician.'

'Actually, I kind of am. Because I know that my thoughts become things. That's a common saying in the law of attraction, *thoughts become things*.'

George frowned at me.

'Think of it this way,' I tried again. 'The law of attraction says that my thoughts, feelings and actions are constantly creating the world around me. Like if I go through my day in a bad mood, snapping at everyone, I'm creating a shitty day for myself.'

'Yeah, but you didn't create that car.'

'Didn't I? I expected that it would come my way - rather than expecting I'd never be able to afford such a car - and it did come my way.'

'Through hard work,' George argued.

'Of course through hard work! But that mindset of expectation lit a fire under me. It gave me permission to ask for what I want, regardless of how achievable it seemed at the time, and instilled in me a calm confidence that it would happen.'

At its heart, the law of attraction is a way for you to take charge of your thoughts, so that you're in the best frame of mind to achieve . . . well, whatever you want. But how can you harness the law of attraction and turn your *thoughts* into *things*? Let's leave our Rat Racer friend here and explore some practical tips you can employ.

TAKING CHARGE OF YOUR THOUGHTS BY RECOGNISING YOUR FEELINGS

Mastering the law of attraction means learning to master your thoughts. Basically, to consciously choose your thoughts, just as you choose other things in your life, like what to have for breakfast or which film to watch on a Friday night.

One of the most important things you can do is choose positive thoughts.

Of course, it's not possible to monitor every single thought we have. My brain is constantly pinging between thoughts! And they're not all positive all the time. But don't worry, the odd negative thought isn't going to automatically bring negative things your way. You don't have to police every single thought that pops into your head - rather, we're talking about an overall pattern of thought. As in, do you overwhelmingly focus on the positive, the good things in life that you already have and the wonderful things you want in future, or do you overwhelmingly think about things that might go wrong, that you don't want to happen, and so on?

A good way to gauge this is to tap into your feelings. Apologies for another car reference, but your emotions are like the dipstick in an engine. They give you a quick indication of what you're thinking, without having to analyse every little thought.

Feeling relaxed, happy or comfortable? That's a pretty sure sign that you're largely focusing on positive thoughts. Feeling tense, nervous, angry or sad? Well, that's when you know your thoughts are tending towards the negative.

I try to check in with my feelings several times a day, and if I need to, I take steps to shift my emotions to a more positive place - by blasting a song that I love, listening to some positive affirmations (see Chapter 4), looking at pictures of my family, or just thinking of a happy memory.

I also work hard to remove negativity from my life, wherever possible. I surround myself with positive people that lift me up emotionally, not drag me down. I surround myself with people who go after what they want in life. I respectfully correct people when they say I can't do something.

Rewiring your thoughts is one of the best ways to make the law of attraction work for you. But what else can do you to harness this powerful tool? *The Secret* describes a three-step process of Ask, Believe, Receive. Here's what that looks like to the Extraordinary Millionaire . . .

GOALS, GOALS, GOALS

So many of these techniques come back to knowing exactly what you want, and the law of attraction is no different. You must be clear about what you want. If you aren't, how do you expect to manifest it? So, start by working out exactly what it is you really want. Creating a dream board or goal list is a useful way of crystallising what you want into words or images. By becoming clear on what you want, you are starting to attract it to you.

Importantly, not everything that you want to manifest has to be a big, crazy goal. In fact, a great way to get started with the law of attraction is to focus on manifesting something relatively small. Like me and that car. Okay, a fancy car isn't exactly small fry when it comes to goals, but compared to some of the other things I was gunning for? It seemed the most achievable at the time.

Ultimately, whatever you want to achieve in terms of big, long-term goals, you can't manifest it overnight. You can and you will manifest it, but it may take a while to get there. So I find it really motivating to also manifest short-term and smaller things along the way. By attaining some of the things you want - even the relatively small things - it gives you belief that you can and will manifest the bigger things over time.

In this way, try to come up with some smaller goals that can act as stepping stones on your law of attraction journey. It could be anything: a better job, a new bathroom, a holiday, a perfect date with a lovely person, lower blood pressure, losing half a stone, calmer mornings, better sleep, you name it.

It's also important to recognise that some things will be a more pressing priority at different stages of your life. I really wanted that car when I was younger and living the free and single lifestyle. As I got older, I found I wanted to manifest different things, like that dream family home and presenting a TV programme.

There's something I've had on my dream board for years and years, something that I haven't yet manifested, because it's not the right time for me to do so. It's a slipper launch, one of those beautiful wooden pleasure boats you see on the Thames. It's a posh man's boat, basically. It's hardly a superyacht - truth be told, I could have afforded to buy myself a slipper launch at any time in the last decade. But, much as I'd love to have one, it's not a priority for me at this point in my life. I see myself having this boat when I'm older, when the kids are older, when my wife and I have more time to enjoy being out on the water. I'm not going to take it off my dream board or stop imagining myself with that boat. I know for certain it'll come into my life when the time is right. But, for now, there are higher priorities for me to manifest.

Bottom line, give yourself a variety of things that you want to manifest - short-term, long-term, big, small, medium . . . You can focus on one goal at a time, or pick a few. Then simply tune your thoughts towards that thing (or things) you want. Visualise it happening, using the practical steps in Chapter 2.

Don't think about what you *don't* want, or all the things that may stand in the way of achieving your goal. Just keep focusing on the amazing outcome that's coming your way.

TRUST IN THE UNIVERSE

Deciding what you want and visualising it with all your might is a start. Next you need to trust that it will be yours. Cultivate a feeling of certainty that what you want is definitely coming your way, and relax into that certainty.

So, for now, don't worry about the specifics of how you'll achieve your goal. You don't need to know everything right away. This is difficult to achieve for lots of people, as we naturally want to control our circumstances, and, when things are uncertain, it can be hard to believe in the end result. But that's exactly what you have to do for the law of attraction to work - you must be absolutely certain that you will get what you want. Not a fraction of doubt.

At the time, I didn't know where I would find the money to get that Nissan GTR. But it didn't matter. I knew it would come to me, eventually. I nurtured the feeling that it was all going to work out, and that certainty was an incredibly empowering feeling. Especially at that point in my life, when my mental health was at its lowest ebb.

That's an important point to remember about the law of attraction. It's so often referred to as a way to attain success and wealth, but it's also a brilliant mental health tool. It certainly was for me.

Admittedly, it takes a lot of confidence to let go and trust that things will come your way. Especially if that's not been your experience so far in life. But continue to work at it and you'll build confidence in your ability to manifest the things you desire.

LIVE THE LIFE YOU WANT

A big part of the law of attraction is thinking, speaking and acting like you've already achieved your goal. In other words, living the life you want right now.

When I was in that flat in Dover, I didn't have a lot of cash to throw around. But I lived with a prosperous mindset. I thought of myself as a successful person. I spoke, not of the things I didn't have, but of the things I had and would have. I acted with confidence, as though I'd already made it, even though I hadn't. In short, I moved through each day with the attitude of a successful business person, and that's what I ultimately became.

More than that, I *felt* as though I'd made it. Regardless of what my bank statements said, I felt like a rich person, living an abundant life. And so should you.

Whatever you're aiming for, feel as though you're already there. Feel like you're in perfect health. Feel like you've secured your dream job. Feel like you've found your soulmate. Feel all those feelings of joy and satisfaction that come from achieving your goal - because, when you feel good, you attract good things. Again, visualisation (Chapter 2) can be a really powerful way to tap into those feelings of achieving your goals.

LIVING IN ABUNDANCE

This is ultimately what we're talking about, living in abundance. Living like a millionaire, even when you're not (yet).

Easy for you to say, you might be thinking. Because, yes, I am a millionaire . . . now. But I haven't always been. I didn't grow up wealthy. In fact, there have been times when I've been downright broke. But I've always tried to live with abundance in mind.

I'm not talking about splashing the cash left, right and centre. I'm talking about having an abundant mindset, where you focus on what you have and what you want, not all the things you lack.

Here's a good example. So many people who struggle financially focus on their bills and costs. They try to reduce their costs to have more money. Successful people, people with an abundant mindset, think of generating more money, not trimming their costs. But we'll get to the money side of things later in this story.

It's really important to live with this abundant attitude because it also filters down to your children, if you have them. My children see this sort of attitude as normal because they live with it every day. My wife and I are teaching them, through our actions, how to live with the law of attraction and abundance in mind. They're not spoilt. They have to work for the things they want, but they're learning to focus on those things instead of the things they don't have in life.

As such, we're always having conversations with our kids along the lines of, 'If you believe you can do it, you will. But if you believe you're going to fail, you will.'

A good way to live with abundance in mind is to practise gratitude (see Chapter 4). Indeed, gratitude is a key part of the law of attraction. When you feel grateful for the things you already have in life - from the small things to the big things - you're better able to maintain a positive mindset, which, in turn, attracts more good things to you. It's a great way to shift your feelings and bring about more of what you want in life.

GIVE BACK TO GET MORE

Let's return to that notion of 'you get back what you put out there'. Because, when you really start delving into the law of attraction, you realise old sayings like this - sayings that we hear all the time but never give much thought to - are 100% rooted in the truth. So the next time you hear someone saying 'you get back what you put out there', remember it's not just a saying; it connects to a very practical technique, the law of attraction.

And what are you putting out there? Thoughts, obviously. Words. Behaviours. What about money?

It may seem counterintuitive, but giving money away brings more prosperity to you, not less. By giving money - however little - you're saying 'I have plenty'. Because those who give to others get more back in return. By saying you can't afford to give, you're only attracting more of the same. So it's no surprise that people like Bill Gates and Warren Buffet, some of the richest people in the world, are some of the world's biggest philanthropists.

However, giving back isn't just about donating money. Are you putting your time, energy and attention out there? Are you giving back to your community, your industry or your customers, whether it's through mentoring, volunteering, reading at the local primary school, or whatever?

Living in abundance isn't just about living like a millionaire; it's about living as though you have a wealth of time and energy and attention for those people and causes that matter to you. Just as saying 'I can't afford to give money' only attracts more money worries your way, saying things like 'I don't have time' attracts more time pressure your way.

I'm usually spinning a lot of plates at any one time, but when a friend of mine was setting off to deliver supplies to Ukrainian refugees in Poland - this was just after the Russian invasion had started - I dropped everything to go and help. Literally, we spoke on the phone about his trip, and how he was going to be driving across Europe on his own, and within the hour I was rounding up unwanted toys and clothes from my kids, packing a bag, and joining him in his van. We spent two days driving to Poland, where we met with our contact and delivered all the supplies my friend had rounded up. At the shelter, I choked up as I handed one of my daughter's stuffed animals to a little Ukrainian girl whose family had lost everything. It was humbling and devastating and life-affirming all at the same time. And to think I could so easily have said, 'I wish I could help but I'm really busy . . .'

In a similar way, when you're doing well, hoarding that success for yourself - worrying that others might take a piece of your pie - is counterintuitive according to the law of attraction. Because if you worry about losing what you have, you're more likely to attract that very thing. There's plenty of success to go around for everyone. When you adopt that attitude, you attract more success and abundance to yourself.

That's why one of my businesses, the Property Forum, provides lots of free advice to help people get started in property investing and build a successful career in property. I've no intention of keeping the secrets of successful property investing to myself. That's not the way to attract more success. That's not living with abundance.

This all feeds into the law of attraction because, by giving back to others, you're saying thank you. Thank you for everything I have in my life that allows me to give to others. It's a really powerful way to supercharge the law of attraction.

PUTTING THE WORK IN

For the law of attraction to work, you need to live these steps daily. You need to tune into your thoughts and feelings, reaffirm your goals and visualise what you want. You need to think, speak and act like you have the life you desire. You need to catch yourself when you start to say something negative and instead turn it into a positive. You need to trust that you will manifest the things you want. You need to live with abundance in mind.

And you need to keep doing all that until it becomes second nature.

Maybe you won't get instant results (although some people claim they do). But keep at it and you will see results. And the more you see results, the greater your confidence will be in this process, which will deliver even greater results.

Most importantly, though, you need to take steps towards the things you want. The law of attraction is a powerful technique that helps you create the ideal mindset for success, but it's not a shortcut to an amazing life. You have to put the work in and move in the direction of your goals. As Jim Carrey, a big believer in the law of attraction, put it, 'You can't just visualise and then go eat a sandwich!'

To get my Nissan GTR, I had to gradually build my passive income from rental properties until it was enough to comfortably cover the monthly payments on such a car. (Yes, I got that fancy car on finance! I didn't amass the money to buy it outright. I was manifesting what I wanted long before I became a millionaire.)

It was only a car but it meant so much to me. It cemented my feelings of living in abundance and being a successful entrepreneur, even though I was still living in that crappy flat in Dover. I had manifested something from my dream board, and I was hungry to manifest the next success. It was like a snowball effect, because potential investors saw me turning up in my nice car and recognised that I was obviously doing alright. Or maybe it was just my attitude. Maybe that car gave me more confidence in my abilities. It doesn't matter - I was well on my way.

HOW *NOT* TO MANIFEST

The law of attraction works both ways, in that you can attract good things your way, or not-so-good things. What you think about, comes about. Like attracts like.

Again, I'm not saying that if you have one negative thought you'll instantly manifest something bad. But your overall pattern of thought certainly shapes how you move through life, the opportunities you attract, and the outcomes you achieve. If you go through life thinking you'll never amount to anything, you'll undoubtedly prove yourself right.

So the biggest mistake in terms of the law of attraction is focusing your thoughts in the wrong direction: on lack rather than abundance, on what you don't want instead of what you do want. There's an Oprah Winfrey quote that sums it up perfectly: 'Be thankful for what you have; you'll end up having more. If you concentrate on what you don't have, you will never, ever have enough.'

It's like my Rat Racer friend saying things like, 'I can't afford to quit my job' or 'I've got bills to pay'. Those things may be true, but thinking those thoughts, speaking that way and acting with those thoughts in mind wasn't serving him. It didn't help him move towards what he really wanted, which was to be a successful entrepreneur.

How would I reframe such thoughts, if it were me? I'd tell myself that I lived an abundant life, that success flows my way, that I can do anything I put my mind to.

I'd also think the kind of thoughts that allow me to be happy in the here and now, to be more present and grateful. But more on that in the coming chapters.

THIS STUFF WORKS

The law of attraction isn't a shortcut to wealth and happiness. You have to put the work in. You have to take charge of your thoughts and feelings.

You have to act with your goals in mind. But if you do that - if you live with the law of attraction in mind - you can manifest the things you want. Just as I manifested that car.

Later in life, it was exactly the same with my TV programme. That was the culmination of a huge life goal that I'd been working towards for years. I'd been building my brand and my network. I'd been forming relationships with people who could help me achieve that goal. I'd been working on my skills as an educator, writing content and putting out YouTube videos. I did all that. But I also firmly believe that the law of attraction brought that goal closer to me.

Because it taught me that my thoughts, feelings and actions create the world around me. This simple truth kept me on track. It kept me focused on positive thoughts, emotions and behaviour - exactly what I want to receive back. It boosted my mental health, too, because, safe in the knowledge that I could and would achieve everything I wanted, I stopped stressing so much about the future. The law of attraction ensured I didn't give in to uncertainty.

And all of this helped me perform better at work, which in turn helped me attract bigger investors, bigger projects and better relationships my way. In other words, the law of attraction kept me on the path to success.

LAW OF ATTRACTION LESSONS FROM THE RAT RACER AND THE EXTRAORDINARY MILLIONAIRE

- The Rat Racer doesn't realise they're a magnet, attracting the things they think about most.
- The Extraordinary Millionaire knows that they create the world around them through their thoughts, feelings, and actions. They know that thoughts become things and like attracts like. They know that you get back what you put out there.
- Someone with a Rat Racer mindset will dwell more on what they

don't want to happen, the bad things that have happened in the past, and all the things they don't have.

- The Extraordinary Millionaire tunes their thoughts to all the good things they have in their life, and all the good things that are coming their way. They consciously choose their thoughts like they choose which T-shirt to wear.
- When they do think of what they want, the Rat Racer's thoughts automatically go to all the things that may stand in their way.
- The Extraordinary Millionaire trusts that what they want is coming to them. They expect to receive the things they want most.
- The Rat Racer thinks, speaks and acts from a place of lack instead of abundance.
- The Extraordinary Millionaire thinks like a millionaire regardless of what their bank balance says. They cultivate feelings of abundance. They think, feel and act as though they already have the things they want.
- Someone with a Rat Racer mindset says and thinks things like 'I can't afford to give to charity' or 'I don't have time for that.'
- The Extraordinary Millionaire knows that by saying 'I have plenty' - time, energy, money, whatever - you get back more. By giving back, and by giving thanks, you get more of the things you want.

Positive thinking is a huge part of the law of attraction, but not everyone is a natural optimist. So let's pull out our next tool in the mindset toolkit - thinking like an optimist, even if you're not one . . .

Chapter 4

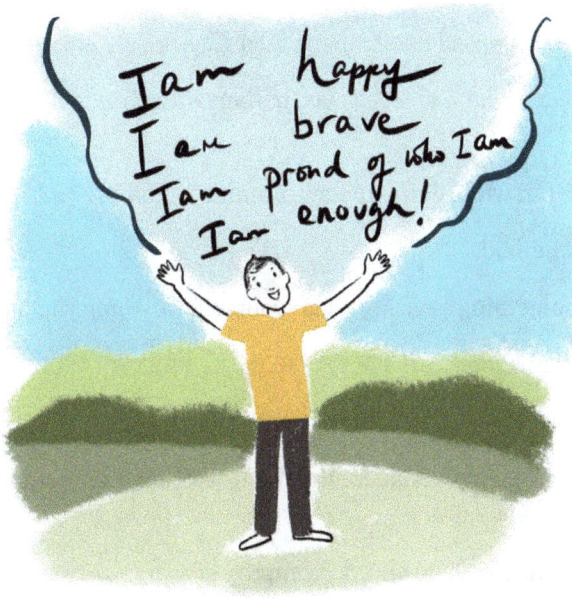

**Thinking Like an Optimist –
Even if You're Not One**

We were barbecuing at a local beauty spot, a joint day out for my family and our friends from next door. Rain earlier in the day seemed to have kept most other people away, and we had the whole picnic clearing, next to country park woodland, to ourselves. Apart from a dog walker, we hadn't seen anyone in the last hour.

'Go on,' I nodded at my daughter. 'There's no one around.'

She smiled shyly. 'Nooo. Someone might hear. You do it.'

'Alright then,' I said. I turned to face the empty woodland and yelled at the top of my lungs, 'I AM THE BEST VERSION OF ME!'

My daughter collapsed into embarrassed giggles.

Our Rat Racer friend wandered over, barbecue tongs in his hand. 'What's going on?'

'Just a little fun while there's no one around,' I said. 'Try it.'

'Try what?' he said.

'Shouting something amazing about yourself. Anything you like.'

He thought for a moment. 'I'M THE BEST . . . BARBECUE CHEF?'

It sounded more like a question than a statement.

My daughter laughed again. 'You're doing it wrong,' she said. 'You have to say it like you believe it.'

'Maybe you should show him,' I prompted her.

She went all shy again.

'Who's the best?' I asked her.

'I am,' she replied automatically. We'd had this back-and-forth her whole life, just as my father had done with me.

I nodded towards the woodland.

'I'M THE BEST I CAN BE!' she shouted, before collapsing into more giggles.

'You guys are nuts,' neighbour George shook his head and went back to his hot dogs.

'Yeah, but we're the best at it,' I replied.

THE MIND IS A POWERFUL THING

Actually, I wasn't so sure that we *were* nuts. Because as the law of attraction teaches us, positivity attracts more positivity our way. If there are practical ways to bring about a more positive mindset - whether it's shouting something affirming about yourself or taking a quiet moment of positive reflection - it would be nuts to *not* use those tools.

That day in the woods, I was reminding my children that the mind is a powerful force that not only influences how we feel physically and emotionally - it creates the world around us. That's what the law of attraction teaches us, after all. What we think about comes about.

It's not that George was an outright pessimist, as such. But he hadn't really given much attention to the importance of positive thinking, and how to use it to his advantage. Here's how I made the case for positive thinking.

'George, have you ever thought about a particular car and then started seeing that car everywhere? In front of you on the motorway, parked next to you at the supermarket, in TV and magazine adverts . . . It's not like the number of cars of this make and model have multiplied overnight. It's just that your brain has tuned in and focused on that specific car, and you're now much more aware of it around you.'

He thought for a moment. 'Weirdly, that happened to me recently. Not with a car, but with Sicily. We watched this TV programme set there, and I thought how much I'd love to take the family there one day. Then that was it, Sicily kept popping up everywhere. In a podcast I was listening to. On Instagram. That sort of thing.'

'It's the same with positive thinking,' I said. 'When you think positive thoughts, when you're tuned in to that positivity, chances are you'll see, hear and experience more positive things around you. Strangers seem more smiley than usual on your morning commute. You're able to focus on the good news stories, instead of dwelling on the bad ones. All this makes you feel more positive and the cycle continues.'

In this way, positive thinking is not just a tool for coping with the more challenging aspects of life; it's a way to create the world we want to see around us. It's a lesson that I try to teach my kids every day.

'It makes sense,' George mused. 'But you talk about positive thinking like it's some sort of practical skill. Like learning to change a tyre or speak a new language.'

'Because it *is* a practical skill,' I said. 'On a small scale, positive thinking can help you mentally prepare for the day ahead, or a particular event - like a meeting that you've been anxious about. By focusing on the positive outcome that you want from your day, you're tuning your mind and creating the ideal conditions for achieving that outcome. And on a larger scale, you can use positive thinking to focus on goals that you want to achieve. If you believe you won't amount to anything in life, or that your business will fail, you'll get what you focus on. But, if you tune your mind to positive thoughts of you as a successful business owner, you're more likely to be aware of and open to opportunities that deliver that goal - just like being more aware of that car or Sicily suddenly popping up everywhere.'

'WHETHER YOU THINK YOU CAN, OR YOU THINK YOU CAN'T, YOU'RE RIGHT·'

This quote by Henry Ford really resonated with me. Because, when I quit my comfortable, lucrative job to pursue a new life as a property entrepreneur I could so easily have thought, 'I can't do this.' After all, I knew nothing about property, or running a business for that matter, and all I had in my bank account was enough cash to get me through one month. One month!

Safe to say my decision raised more than a few eyebrows among those who knew me. At that point, I didn't know my Rat Racer friend. It was 2002. I was living elsewhere, and hadn't yet met my wife or started a family. But I know my Rat Racer friend would have thought what a lot of other people thought at the time - that I was probably going to fail.

I, on the other hand, just *knew* I was going to succeed. I told myself every single day that it was going to be okay. Better than okay, in fact - I told myself over and over again that I was going to achieve everything I ever wanted. I had a relentless desire to be successful, and a relentless belief in my own abilities to create that success. I had no foundation for this belief whatsoever - no entrepreneurial experience, no training, and no comfortable wad of cash as a cushion. But that didn't matter to me. I had total faith in my abilities, and an underlying confidence and determination that meant I wasn't afraid of leaving my comfortable job.

It's not like I consciously said to myself, 'What I need is a bit of positive thinking.' There wasn't anything conscious about it. I just knew on a deep level that if I told myself I was going to fail, then that's what would happen. Telling myself I would make it was the only way of ensuring I actually *would* make it. Over time, this evolved into a more structured approach, where I'd do certain practices every day to help me stay positive.

I recounted all this to George and he replied, 'Yeah, but it's easy for you. You're obviously one of life's optimists.'

'I am in the sense that I prefer to think of all the things that will go right, rather than all the things that might go wrong. But even I have to put a bit of work in and make time for positive thinking. Even if you're not one of life's optimists, you can still benefit from a structured practice of positive thinking.'

'A structured practice?' George asked. His tone of voice suggested I had asked him to climb Mount Everest or take on a similarly mammoth task.

'Don't get me wrong, I'm not talking about spending lots of time and energy on this. I just mean using quick and practical tools on a regular basis to help tune the brain to more positive thoughts. Positive affirmations and gratitude are my go-to tools.'

'Gratitude, I get,' George said. 'Gratitude is a positive feeling. But you're going to have to explain the whole affirmations thing. Sounds like hippy nonsense to me.'

WHAT YOU TELL YOURSELF (AND YOUR KIDS) MATTERS

It was a bit of fun, shouting into the trees on our family day out, but the underlying sentiment was 100% serious.

When my brother and I were young, my dad used to say to us, 'We are Wallworks, and we are the best'. He didn't mean it in an arrogant way, although I see how it might come across that way on paper. It was a simple one-sentence distillation of larger lessons that he was constantly teaching us - that whatever we chose to do and be in life, we could be the best at it. That we could be the best possible versions of ourselves. That we could be the best people we could possibly be. That everything we needed was already inside us.

I told George this story and concluded, 'That was my first experience of positive affirmations. Not that my dad ever called it an affirmation. It was just something he said to us all the time. But an affirmation is exactly what it was.'

'It's just a statement,' George said.

'Well, it's a statement that motivates and inspires you. It could be anything, from general mood-lifters, like "I'm the best version of me" to specific phrases, like "I'm a confident public speaker." That sort of thing. I'm not the only one who loves affirmations, by the way. When Muhammad Ali said, "I am the greatest" that was a positive affirmation. Michelle Obama tells herself daily that she is good enough.'

'It's just words,' George said.

'But words matter!' I argued. 'What we tell ourselves matters. Haven't you ever thought to yourself, "I did a good job on that" or "I look nice in this" or something like that?'

'Of course,' he replied.

'And didn't it affect how you felt, in a good way?'

'Sure. But what's the point of telling myself I'm a confident public speaker, to take your example, if I'm not one?'

'Because the very act of saying those words - and believing them - can help you become the person you want to be. Of course, if you've no interest in becoming a better public speaker, then that affirmation isn't the best use of your time. But if it's important to you to succeed at that goal, affirmations will help. Let me put it this way, if your kid fell off her bike the first time she rode it, and immediately said she couldn't do it, what would you tell her?'

'I'd tell her that she could,' he said.

'Exactly. Why would you tell yourself something different?'

As I've said before, I didn't grow up wealthy. Comfortable, yes, but not well off. But my dad's often-repeated affirmation was worth more than anything. It had a profound effect on me, even from a very young age. It gave me great confidence. It told me I could achieve anything I wanted, and that I could excel at whatever I put my mind to. Anyone who had a parent or teacher tell them something similar will immediately understand how important it is to hear that kind of message. I make sure my kids hear similar messages all the time - that they can be anything they want, that they're the best versions of themselves. I get them to say it back to me. I hope they'll do the same thing with their own children one day.

In this way, affirmations are a great way to shift your mood if you're in need of a boost. But more than that, affirmations help you work towards your bigger life goals and achieve success, whatever that looks like to you. As bestselling author Hal Elrod puts it, 'Affirmations are one of the most effective tools for quickly becoming the person you need to be to achieve everything you want in your life.'

Affirmations are one of my favourite ways of cutting through the distractions of everyday life and boosting positivity. Another thing I've noticed is affirmations help me to be more focused. To be successful at anything - Olympic gymnast, property developer, anything - you have to be extremely focused. Incorporating affirmations into my daily routine brings a structure and focus to my thoughts, putting me in the right frame of mind for success. Basically, affirmations stop my busy mind from wandering. They help keep the noise out, keep me on track, and keep me laser-focused on my goals. And as a bonus, when I feel focused, I feel more positive about the day ahead.

Regardless of where you sit on the optimist-pessimist spectrum, affirmations will help you get into a more positive mindset, believe in your ability to achieve whatever you want in life, and even overcome challenges that come your way. So how can you, reader, build a regular practice of positive affirmations?

DECIDING YOUR AFFIRMATIONS

No one can tell you exactly what to say to yourself, as we all have different motivations and different things that we want to achieve. The key is to find affirmations that resonate with you, whether they're very specific statements or general statements that inspire success.

You can borrow and adapt affirmations from people you admire, or borrow from the many books, websites and apps that are tailored to affirmations. You can, of course, develop your own statements that are completely unique and personal to you. I recommend using the ThinkUp app, because it gives tons of example affirmations you can use, and lets you create your own. (Another good thing about this is it lets you record your own voice saying your affirmations, so you can play them back whenever you like. Apparently, hearing your own voice saying information, as opposed to just reading it on a page, makes it more likely that the information will stick in your brain . . .)

If you're new to affirmations, a good place to start is with 'I am' statements that affirm what you want to be or feel. 'I am successful' is a simple one. 'I am the best version of me' is lovely. Other examples include:

- I am happy.
- I am brave.
- I am proud of who I am.
- I am confident.
- I am inspired.
- I am enough.

You don't have to start your affirmations with 'I am', and you can get really quite specific with what you say. For example, you can create affirmations that tie into specific goals.

'I am ready to become a successful entrepreneur' would have been a great one for my Rat Racer friend, if he were open to using affirmations. Or 'I have the courage to start my own business.' Or even 'I attract the things I want. Exciting business opportunities flow my way.'

Sometimes, I'll use affirmations to plan for a successful day or week ahead. For example, I might start my day by saying something like, 'Today I will write 1,000 words on my book' or 'What will make this week great is achieving X, Y and Z.' Or if I have a really important meeting coming up that day, I might say something like, 'I am well prepared and ready for this meeting.'

Affirmations like this help me to get clarity on the day and week ahead, and focus on what I want to happen, as opposed to getting bogged down in the things I *don't* want to happen. In this way, affirmations are a really useful way to boost your law of attraction and visualisation practices - by simply verbalising the things you want, as well as visualising them.

That's an important thing to note. Just as with the law of attraction, you should be verbalising what you want, rather than what you don't want. Never use 'I don't' or 'I won't' or 'I'm not' phrases. 'I won't mess up my presentation,' isn't a positive affirmation; it's a negative one.

Over time, you'll probably amass quite a long list of positive affirmations that you can pick and choose from depending on how you're feeling or what you want to achieve.

Using the ThinkUp app, I've organised my favourite affirmations into categories such as:

- Motivation
- Energy
- Helping others
- Calm
- Self-esteem
- Leading my team

So, for example, under the motivation category, I have affirmations like 'Don't ask why this is happening *to* me, ask why is this happening *for* me.' (My life coach gave me that one, and I've found it a really powerful phrase to use when life throws obstacles my way. It's far more practical and motivating than those general platitudes we hear all the time, like 'Everything happens for a reason' or 'Every cloud has a silver lining.')

And under the calm category, for those days when I'm not feeling particularly calm but I really want to, I have affirmations like 'Calmness washes over me with every deep breath I take' and 'I am calm and relaxed in all situations.'

I pick from the categories according to how I'm feeling on that day, or depending on what I want to achieve. This is one of the things I love about affirmations - they're so flexible, and you can tailor them to suit pretty much any situation, desire or goal.

In other words, don't think of your affirmations as being set in stone. You can update and tailor them every day if it helps you. In fact, I find they're more powerful when I *don't* repeat the exact same thing every day, and you may find the same. You can tailor them to suit your mood - so, if you're feeling anxious, use affirmations that boost your confidence or lift your mood, and if you're feeling happy and excited about something, use affirmations that build on that energy and excitement.

MAKING AFFIRMATIONS WORK FOR YOU

The good news is you don't have to go and stand in nature and yell your affirmations at the top of your lungs for them to work. You can say them quietly to yourself, or just think them to yourself if you prefer.

It does help, though, to write your affirmations down, either on paper, in your phone, or using an app. You can write complete statements, like 'I am calm and relaxed in all situations.' You can also write prompts, such as 'I am____' leaving a blank space for you to fill in according to what you want to happen or how you feel that day. The important thing is to have them written down somewhere, so you can quickly get into the right headspace, without sitting there scratching your head and wondering what to say.

Having them written down also helps to keep it fresh, because you can have a broader range of affirmations to choose from - like me and my different categories - rather than just saying the same one sentence over and over every single day, which would quickly become boring and lose its power.

If possible, try to get into the habit of saying your affirmations at the same time every day, whether that's first thing in the morning, in the shower, or whenever. You can also say them throughout the day or when you need a confidence boost - just before you go into that critical meeting, for example. The important thing isn't where or when you say them, but that you make it part of your daily routine. As with all of these Extraordinary Millionaire mindset techniques, repetition is key. You want this to become second nature.

A big part of making affirmations work for you, aside from making it a daily habit, is learning to believe in yourself and, crucially, believe in your affirmations. Just as with visualisation and the law of attraction, you have to wholeheartedly believe in an affirmation for it to have any real effect. So, you can't just say 'Money and success flows to me' while inside you're thinking nothing will ever go your way. As my daughter explained to our Rat Racer neighbour, you have to believe the things you're saying will happen. You have to believe you'll achieve everything you desire.

You have to mean what you're saying, basically. So try to cultivate those feelings that accompany the words. If you're telling yourself you're successful and confident, conjure up those feelings. If you're telling yourself you are calm and relaxed, take deep breaths and work on actually *feeling* it.

Over time, it becomes a self-fulfilling prophecy: having total confidence in your affirmation delivers confidence in life, which means good things are more likely to come your way, thereby boosting your confidence in your affirmations. And so it continues.

'BE THANKFUL FOR WHAT YOU HAVE; YOU'LL END UP HAVING MORE.'

This Oprah quote perfectly sums up the importance of gratitude. Along with affirmations, practising gratitude is one of the best ways to cultivate a more positive mindset.

It's also a key part of making the law of attraction work for you. When you feel grateful for the things you already have in life - from the small things to the big things - you're attracting more good things your way. If you only ever think of all the things you don't have, you'll never have enough.

It's so important to be grateful for what you have in your life *right now* - even if it seems like you don't have a great deal. I've been there, living in that crappy flat in Dover and struggling to make ends meet as I got my property business off the ground. But I found that being grateful even for very small things - like a message from an old friend - helped me attract more good things into my life. Because gratitude is an immensely powerful positive emotion.

Being thankful is also a fantastic way to shut out the noise of everyday life and bring calm in the present. It helps you let go of stresses and anxieties about the day or week ahead. Focusing on the good things in life, whether it's family, friends, an achievement you're proud of, a presentation that went well, or anything else that you're thankful for, sets you up for a happier, calmer, more positive day.

I start each morning by giving thanks for the things that I'm grateful for. This changes from day to day and may include my beautiful family, my friends, finishing my latest book, an exciting new business opportunity that's in the pipeline, or simply good health. I think about how lucky I am to live the life I do, and I experience a feeling of profound gratitude. For me, it's a great way to supercharge my feelings of positivity as I face the day.

Rhonda Byrne, author of *The Secret*, goes even further and repeats 'thank you' out loud over and over again. As she gets out of bed she says 'thank you', as she showers she says 'thank you'. She says 'thank you' hundreds of times just while getting ready in the morning. She says, 'There is no more powerful way to begin your day than this.'

Whether you go as far as Rhonda Byrne and say 'thank you' hundreds of times a day, or just spend a quite few minutes thinking of things you're grateful for, I strongly recommend you make gratitude a part of your daily routine. By tuning your mind to the more positive aspects of life, whatever they may be, you'll be more aware of and open to positive things around you.

Do this even when life isn't going the way you want. Especially when life isn't going the way you want . . .

GETTING YOUR DAILY HAPPINESS INJECTION

Here's how to turn the simple act of feeling grateful into an easily-repeatable daily practice.

Start each day by saying or thinking three things that you're grateful for. You can be thankful for small, specific things, like an upcoming lunch with a friend you haven't seen in ages, or huge things like good health or that your kids are happy. I feel instantly brighter when I start my day this way.

Try to keep it fresh by being thankful for different things each morning. Again, this is where affirmations can come in handy, because you can create a list of gratitude-related affirmations to use as and when you like. Some of my gratitude affirmations include:

- I'm grateful for the good in my life.
- I love the life I have whilst I work towards the life of my dreams.
- I experience gratitude deeply.

Having got your morning happiness injection, keep the good vibes going by saying 'thank you' throughout the day when things go well. Got a parking space right outside the office? Say 'thank you' in your head. A friend sent you a message that made you smile? Say 'thank you' to yourself (and to your friend). Your lunchtime sandwich had extra cheese? 'Thank you!' It sounds silly, but this practice of saying thank you drastically opens up your awareness, meaning you'll start to notice more and more positive things happening around you. Try it today. Try saying thank you for lots of little things, and marvel at how many other positive little things you notice.

Buy yourself a nice notebook to keep by your bed and use as a gratitude journal. Then every night before you go to sleep, write down three things that made your day great. Could be anything. A happy client, something thoughtful that your partner did, your child's awesome school report. Anything at all. Looking back through your journal from time to time - especially if you need an emotional boost - will only make you feel more grateful.

THE OLD 'I DON'T HAVE TIME FOR THAT' ARGUMENT

George wasn't a doom-and-gloom pessimist, but he didn't see the value of creating a daily practice of positivity. When I described my morning routine of affirmations and gratitude, he just shook his head and said he didn't have time for all that in the mornings.

I got where he was coming from. It was a mission for my family to get out the door on time each morning.

But the truth is, we make time for the things that matter, don't we? George made time for his Saturday morning cycle club, even though it took up precious weekend time. I make time for things like affirmations and visualisation most mornings, even though there are a million and one other things I could be doing. I only have to get up five minutes earlier to make this happen. It's only five minutes. In the grand scheme of things, that's an easy win.

Yes, it does take work. Training your brain to tune into positivity is like learning any other skill. It takes dedication, effort, and most of all, repetition. You can't learn to speak another language by only doing it once every six months, and the same is true of positive thinking.

It's not always easy to find the time to develop this precious skill, but ideally it should become part of your everyday routine, like remembering to brush your teeth and put on shoes before leaving the house. I wouldn't leave the house without brushing my teeth, and I wouldn't leave the house without my little injection of positivity. It gets me ready to face the day with confidence. It puts me in the right frame of mind for success.

Perhaps even more importantly, positive affirmations and gratitude help me manage my mental health. These tools have helped me through low points just as much as they've helped me achieve new highs. In good days and bad, these are vital tools to have up your sleeve.

POSITIVITY LESSONS FROM THE RAT RACER AND THE EXTRAORDINARY MILLIONAIRE

- Someone with a Rat Racer mindset may believe you're either an optimist or a pessimist. Nothing you can do about it. You can't change how your brain works.
- The Extraordinary Millionaire knows that anyone can learn to steer their thinking in a more positive direction, especially with practical tools like affirmations and gratitude. Because they know that

positive thinking helps them cope with life challenges, create the world around them, and achieve their goals.

- The Rat Racer doesn't catch his negative thoughts and try to turn them into positives. He doesn't realise what he tells himself matters.
- The Extraordinary Millionaire knows that if you tell yourself you're going to fail, you probably will.
- The Rat Racer rolls their eyes at the phrase 'positive affirmations' and mutters something about hippies under their breath.
- The Extraordinary Millionaire knows that these simple, positive phrases are hugely motivating and inspiring. They provide focus and confidence.
- The Rat Racer experiences gratitude when things are going great.
- The Extraordinary Millionaire makes time every day for gratitude. They give thanks for the big and small things in their life, even when life isn't going to plan. They know that if they focus on the good things in life, more good things will come their way.
- The Rat Racer doesn't prioritise time for daily mood-boosting habits.
- The Extraordinary Millionaire makes time. Just a few minutes in the morning and evening delivers amazing results.

Another important way to feel more positive is to tune into the present using meditation and mindfulness. Which brings us to our next Extraordinary Millionaire mindset technique . . .

Chapter 5

Making Mindfulness and Meditation
Work For You

Two men sat side by side on a lake bank. One was sipping coffee from a flask, head tilted towards the dappled sunlight coming through the trees. The other was still, watching for the tell-tale bob of the float on the water's surface.

Eventually, one of the men broke the silence. 'Do you realise we haven't said a word for a good half an hour?'

I broke my gaze away from the lake's surface and smiled at my Rat Racer friend George.

He was right. After setting up our fishing rods and getting comfy in our folding chairs, we'd soon settled into contented silence. Every now and then we'd hear the low hum of a car on the nearby country lane. But otherwise, the only sounds were birdsong and the odd gentle splash.

'Yeah, I can see why you like fishing,' George added. 'There are no distractions. It's just *this* and nothing else,' he gestured out to the lake. 'I wish I could do this more often.'

I was glad he liked it. I'd brought him here not because I needed the company - I was used to fishing alone because my wife thought it was boring as heck and the kids were still too young (and manic) to enjoy it. No, I'd brought George here because *he* needed it. He needed to tune into the here and now.

We were still neighbours, although by this point my wife and I had started looking for our dream home. George and his wife were going through a particularly stressful period: they had a third baby on the way, George's employer was piling on the pressure, and to top it all they were building an extension on their house and doing a lot of the work themselves to save money. He still desperately wanted out of the rat race but, more than ever, seemed stuck in that lane.

So, while his wife and kids decamped to the in-laws for the weekend to escape the dust and debris, I dragged him out to my favourite fishing spot.

I say dragged because he didn't want to come.

'I don't have time, mate,' he said. 'I've got to get these kitchen cabinets in by Monday before the worktop fitters come. Then I've only got Monday and Tuesday evenings to get the tiling finished before I head off for the sales conference on Wednesday. And I haven't even started on my presentation for that.'

'You need a break. Let's go for a couple of hours, then I'll help you finish these cabinets.'

He agreed, reluctantly. But once we'd arrived at the lake, he quickly relaxed into the experience. I could see the tension melt away as he sipped on his coffee and soaked up the peace.

'This is magic,' he said.

'More like mindfulness,' I said.

'Uh-oh, I know where this is going,' he laughed. 'Next thing, you'll have me wearing robes and burning incense.'

THE IMPORTANCE OF NOW

I knew my Rat Racer friend needed a break because he was so focused on the future, reeling off the milestones he had to hit in his renovation schedule to stop the house of cards from tumbling down. I knew the feeling. Before I discovered mindfulness and meditation, I'd often find myself living in the past or the future - dwelling on something that hadn't gone my way or worrying about what would happen next - rather than simply being in the moment. If I was stressed about something, I couldn't just set it aside and enjoy a couple of minutes playing with my kids, because whatever was causing that stress would linger in the back of my mind. Through mindfulness and meditation, I became fully aware of just how little I was living in the present.

There's a popular quote, often attributed to the ancient Chinese philosopher Lao Tzu, that goes, 'If you are depressed, you are living in the past. If you are anxious, you are living in the future. If you are at peace, you are living in the moment.' I used to be rarely at peace but I've honed my skills over the years.

George was not at peace. He was clearly anxious and stressed. But I had an idea of what would help. Because it had helped me.

Mindfulness had helped me to tune my awareness to the present, while meditation taught me to let go of stresses and strains, whether it is the past stress of a difficult project, the present stress of a full inbox or the future stress of a big deadline. Over time, I learned to live more in the moment. More than that, to *enjoy* living in the moment. As such, mindfulness and meditation had become an essential part of looking after my mental health.

I recounted this to George as we sat by the lake that afternoon.

'I have this internal voice,' I said. 'We all do, right? It's telling me what I have to do next, who I have to call, what time I have to be at the next meeting, something I said wrong three years ago . . .'

He nodded in recognition.

'If I let it,' I said, 'that voice will nag at me all day. Then there are all the other distractions going on around me every day: work emails, social media, the busy morning routine getting the family out the door on time, project deadlines, invoices to pay, kids' doctors' appointments. All these things leave little time and energy to focus on what's happening *right now*. So I have to make a conscious choice to focus on the present.'

'Easier said than done,' George said.

'Don't get me wrong, it doesn't come naturally. That's where meditation and mindfulness come in. This right here,' I nodded out to the lake, 'is like a little injection of mindfulness for me. Because when I'm here I'm only really thinking about the present. My mind becomes super-focused on what's going on around me now. It's a gift, really.'

George looked out at the still lake. 'That, I get. But I can't see me getting into all that chanting stuff.'

WHAT'S THE DIFFERENCE BETWEEN MINDFULNESS AND MEDITATION?

Luckily for him, there's no chanting required for either mindfulness or meditation.

'So what is the difference?' he asked.

'Well, they're linked, obviously. Mindfulness can be a form of meditation - in fact, it's my favourite form of meditation - and meditation can be part of living a more mindful life.'

'You've lost me,' he said.

'Mindfulness is being fully aware of the present. It's being aware of your thoughts, feelings and anything else that's going on around you right now. You can be mindful at any minute of the day, just by checking into the here and now. It doesn't have to be anything fancy. You can eat a burger mindfully, just by focusing on each delicious mouthful. Feeling the delicate bun between your fingers, noticing how it feels as your teeth bite through the burger. The smoky taste of the meat, the sweetness of the ketchup. The movement of your jaw as you chew, and so on. To be mindful is to tune out distractions and just be present, without any judgment. So no thinking, "Oh, I'm going to regret this burger" or anything like that. Just notice and pay attention, that's all.'

'Like fishing,' George nodded.

'Exactly. When I cast my line into the water, I'm noticing how the rod feels in my hand. I'm focusing on the water and where I want the line to land. I'm fully present. That's a mindful moment, and you can have those moments at any time, wherever you are or whoever you're with.'

'Isn't meditation just being mindful?' George asked.

'Sort of, in that mindfulness supports meditation. But while you can be mindful informally throughout the day, meditation is usually more of a formal practice. Like mindfulness, meditation involves bringing your attention to something - like the body, or the breath, or an object. Or, dare I say, a mantra, if you're into that sort of meditation. Meditation is basically a brain-training practice, where you're training the mind to achieve calmness.'

I summed it up by saying, 'Basically, mindfulness is more of a feeling of awareness that you can tap into at any moment. Whereas meditation is a more structured practice. It takes a bit more work. But they both support each other, and you can do both, or dip into one or the other depending on what you need, or how much time you have to spare.'

'Clearly you like it,' George said. 'But it's not for everyone is it? It's a bit too "celebrity living in the Hollywood hills with their guru on speed dial" for most people.'

I begged to differ.

THE SCIENTIFIC CASE

'Actually, it was my GP who recommended mindfulness to me,' I corrected him. 'These days, the NHS recommends mindfulness for everything from reducing stress to preventing depression. It's not just some self-help craze. It's evidence based.'

Take a look at the NHS website and you'll notice the benefits of mindfulness include understanding ourselves better, enjoying the world around us more (certainly the case for my neighbour and I while we were at the lake), and coping better with stress and anxiety. In a nutshell, mindfulness allows us to take a step back, recognise how we're feeling and appreciate the present without getting swept up in the past or future.

I've noticed this definitely helps me maintain a more positive mindset, feel more grateful and stay cool, even under intense pressure. Ideally, I'd be mindful every minute of every day, but life just doesn't work out like that. But I've found that just a few minutes of mindfulness across the day reduces my stress and keeps me calm - long after the mindful moment is over.

Likewise, meditation helps me reduce the stresses and anxieties of everyday life. This, in turn, helps me perform better at work and make better decisions – purely because I'm calmer and more focused after meditating. *Hours* after meditating. Days, even. I definitely find meditation makes me feel more positive and motivated. Through meditation, I can take time out to clear my head. I find it's a particularly helpful technique for getting to the root of things that may be bothering me, and, by clearing my mind of distractions, potential solutions or ways forward often reveal themselves more easily.

'But don't take my word for it,' I told George. 'Meditation has been proven to combat stress, anxiety and depression. It's been shown to reinforce memory function, and even help with chronic pain.'

I put it in terms I knew George would identify with. 'Don't you get tired of being constantly "on"? You know, phones pinging with emails, messages, social media and news alerts. It's so hard to switch off these days.'

'I hear you,' he agreed.

'A few minutes without any form of distraction is a precious thing. If I go days without any form of mindfulness or meditation, I start to feel weirdly distanced from myself. I stop noticing how I'm feeling. And I know from experience that's a slippery slope into poor mental health.'

'Listen, on paper it all sounds great,' George said. 'But I'd be lying if I said I was up for sitting cross-legged and going "Om" for ages. It's just not me.'

THE SIMPLER END OF THE MEDITATION SPECTRUM – COMBINING MINDFULNESS AND MEDITATION

'So it sounds like something like transcendental meditation isn't for you then,' I said. 'That's definitely at the more spiritual, religious end of meditation.'

Transcendental meditation is one of the more widely known forms of meditation, largely because it's had a lot of celebrity practitioners over the years, like Sting and the Beatles. It's the form of meditation where you sit with your eyes closed and silently repeat a mantra (typically assigned to you by a trained teacher) for 20 minutes a day.

'Chanting, then,' George said.

'Well, chanting in your head. It's not for me, either,' I admitted. 'I lean more towards mindfulness meditation myself.'

'And that is . . .?'

'Perfect for people like us with a busy brain, or who struggle to sit still for five minutes. It's all about bringing your awareness to your breathing or your body. The body scan is a mindfulness meditation.'

'I've heard of that. I think my son might have done that one at school.'

'I'm not surprised. It's really good for quieting the mind and boosting concentration, so I can see it being perfect for school. All you do is sit or lie in a quiet place, close your eyes and bring your awareness to each part of your body, working your way from the head down to the toes and back again.'

'No robes required,' George said.

'No robes required.'

MEDITATION AND MINDFULNESS IN THE WORKPLACE

I confessed to George that I've even snuck in a quick meditation at work, to improve my performance.

'Seriously,' I said, 'You should try it before you give your presentation at the conference this week. Steve Jobs used to meditate backstage before addressing those huge Apple audiences.'

I explained a quick pre-meeting meditation that I use to help me focus before an important meeting or presentation.

It begins with just sitting quietly, breathing, and noticing how I'm feeling – as in, whether I'm annoyed about something that happened earlier in the day, anxious about the meeting coming up, tense because I have a mountain of emails, and so on. The last thing I want to do is bring those emotions into the meeting. So I just sit quietly, notice those feelings, acknowledge them, then let them go.

And once I'm in the meeting itself, I use mindfulness to help me focus on the present and really listen to others in the room. This means I avoid the temptation to think ahead to the next item on the agenda, to pre-empt what others are about to say, or try and finish their sentences for them. Instead, I can listen deeply. And before I respond, I check back in with my feelings in order to notice where that response might be coming from. I want to respond from a place of clarity and calm, not annoyance or confusion.

Just taking a few mindful or meditative moments before a presentation or meeting has also helped me come up with more creative solutions.

My Rat Racer friend was sceptical.

'Think about it,' I said. 'Have you ever come up with a brilliant idea or solution to a problem just as you were drifting off to sleep?'

'Of course,' George said.

'It's the same thing. We often come up with mental breakthroughs when we're in a more relaxed state. So if I do a quick meditation just before going into a meeting, I'll often come up with more creative solutions and ideas that'll help the meeting.'

I'm not the only one to experience the creative thinking benefits of meditation. Studies have shown that meditation induces states that promote both convergent thinking (generating a solution to a particular problem) and divergent thinking (a way of thinking that helps to generate lots of new ideas). It's no wonder companies like Google and Ford encourage their senior executives to practise meditation and mindfulness.

HOW YOU CAN BE MORE MINDFUL

Now let's explore how you can put these techniques into practice for yourself. Starting with mindfulness.

As I shared with my Rat Racer friend, you can be mindful wherever you are, whatever you're doing and whoever you're with. All you need to do is tune into the present and really focus on how you're feeling in that moment - emotionally and in the body - as well as what's going on around you. It's just about *noticing* more.

You can notice more of the everyday aspects of life. You can notice sensations in your body as you sit in a traffic jam. You can notice your breath in and out as you stand in the shower in the morning. You can notice the sensation of biting into an apple. You can notice the feel of your loved one's hand in yours. Too often we move through life on autopilot, which is a terrible shame. With mindfulness - even just a few moments here and there - we can turn off autopilot mode and re-engage with everyday life.

Trying new things can also help you be more mindful. Even small things like going to a new weekend brunch place, or parking in a different street can help you notice more things around you.

Another good way to be more mindful is to notice your thoughts and feelings across the day. This can be really hard if you're plagued with anxiety because when you quiet the mind, those anxious thoughts and feelings rush in. Mindfulness isn't about eliminating those feelings - rather, it's about noticing them, acknowledging them, and letting them go without judgement. Just as I'd do in my pre-meeting meditation. It might help to name your feelings - such as, 'Oh, that's anxiety' or 'This is me feeling apprehensive about tomorrow's job interview.' Notice it, acknowledge it, then move on.

Most importantly of all, you want to use mindfulness as often as you can. I find it helps to have certain cues that remind me to be more mindful. Fishing is one - when I'm fishing, I know that's a time to tune into the present and block out distractions. I'll turn off my phone, get comfortable, and tune into whatever's going on around me. Practising gratitude and writing in my gratitude journal each night (Chapter 4) is another way of tuning into the present - and it keeps me from reaching for my phone in bed. (Smart phones and social media are the enemy of mindfulness.)

Yoga or tai chi can also help to promote mindfulness, especially for those people with a very busy mind. The movement gives you just enough to focus on to occupy your brain, yet you're also focusing on the sensations of movement and your breath, which is very mindful.

If yoga or tai chi aren't your cup of tea, you could try an app such as Headspace to guide you towards mindful thinking.

Personally, I've found that combining mindfulness with meditation is a great way to build it into a regular routine - something you make time for each morning or night. Which brings us to meditation . . .

GETTING INTO MEDITATION - A FEW POINTERS

We'll get to some practical exercises but, for now, I wanted to cover a few tips that will help you get the most out of meditation.

The first thing I would say is that, just as with mindfulness, meditation should become a regular habit, not something you do every now and then. Generally, I meditate every few days, and I find that's enough for me. You might choose to meditate daily or every other day. I find that meditating in the morning sets me up properly for the day ahead, but you may prefer to meditate at night, or take 10 minutes out of your lunch break. It doesn't matter when, or where or for how long - what matters is that you do it regularly.

Think you don't have time for meditation? That it's just another thing to tag onto the to-do list? Think again. As Arianna Huffington put it, '. . . finding time for meditation was always a challenge because I was under the impression that I had to "do" meditation. And I didn't have time for another burdensome thing to "do". Fortunately, a friend pointed out one day that we don't "do" meditation; meditation "does" us . . . The only thing to "do" in meditation is nothing.'

It's a compelling thought, isn't it, doing *nothing* for a precious few moments?

But if you really do struggle to find five minutes to meditate, you could try doing 'mini meditations' at various points throughout the day. So, if you get a spare moment, just use that time to sit quietly, breathing deeply and focusing on your breath. There's no rule that says meditation only counts if you do it for 20 minutes, or an hour. Even just one minute can help restore a sense of calm in a busy day. I find this is a particularly useful thing to do when something stressful or unexpected arises, or if I'm faced with a tricky problem. It may seem counterintuitive to take a minute to focus on breathing when all hell is breaking loose around you, but, trust me, it'll help you respond in a more thoughtful and constructive way. Turns out the old saying to 'take a deep breath and count to 10' is good advice!

Another important point to note is that meditation isn't an easy thing to master if, like me, you have a busy mind that's always pinging between thoughts. And it's not a quick fix. It takes practice to master meditation and see the benefits, and this is where doing it regularly really helps. It takes quite a few sessions before you begin to feel like you're doing it properly and really start to feel some benefits. So, I recommend you commit to doing it for a while before assessing how it's working for you. You could, for example, try a five-minute meditation every day for a month. (It's easier to maintain focus in shorter sessions when you're just getting started.)

To get the most out of meditation (and mindfulness, for that matter), I recommend using it alongside the other success-building techniques in the Extraordinary Millionaire toolkit, like positive affirmations and visualisation. For example, I'll often go through my affirmations immediately before meditating. (Sometimes, I'll simply sit and repeat an affirmation for a few minutes and that's my meditation.) After meditating, when I feel at my most calm, positive and focused, I might spend a few minutes visualising my goals.

Finally – and this isn't something people often admit about meditating, but it's true – meditation can be a bit, well, boring at first. The first few times I meditated, I found it quite dull, and my mind wandered off in all sorts of directions. If you find the same, I recommend guided audio meditations from apps like Headspace.

With guided meditations, a voice guides you through the practice, bringing your thoughts back to the meditation, which is great for the inexperienced. As you get more experienced, you'll be able to meditate on your own, without anyone guiding you. I started my meditation journey using guided meditations from the Headspace app, and I still use the app even now.

The beauty of having a meditation app is you can practise while you're on the go, away from home, on your lunchbreak or wherever. And you can choose meditations that are relevant to you. Headspace, for example, allows you to select meditations from various categories, so whether you want to feel calmer, boost your self-confidence or whatever, there's a meditation that's perfect for you.

READY TO TRY A FEW SIMPLE MEDITATIONS?

In this section, I explain a couple of easy meditations that I use regularly. But before you get started:

- Switch off your phone (or leave it in another room). And if possible, ask your loved ones not to interrupt you while you're meditating. They can cope without you for 10 minutes.
- Choose a quiet spot and get comfy. For any meditation, you can sit cross-legged on the floor if you like, lie flat on your back, sit in a chair, or whatever works for you. I just sit upright.
- Don't be surprised if various thoughts pop into your head as you meditate. It's very hard to clear your mind of all thoughts completely. Just try to acknowledge each thought, without any frustration or judgement, and then let it go. Gently bring your attention back to your meditation.

Body scan meditation

How about a super-simple body scan meditation to start? I find this quick meditation is perfect for the morning as it gets me feeling calm, focused and ready for the day. It's also great for relieving tension or even helping to manage pain.

- Close your eyes and begin to focus on your breath as you breathe deeply through the nose, pushing out your belly as you breathe in and sucking in the belly as you breathe out. (Basically, breathe from the belly, not the chest.) Continue breathing in this way.
- Bring your awareness to each part of your body and the sensations each part is feeling. Start at the top of your head and work your way down to your toes. Then simply work back in the opposite direction, taking it slowly and really paying attention to each part of your body.
- If you notice any uncomfortable sensations in the body, breathe into them and try to imagine the discomfort or tension evaporating into thin air.

Mindful breathing

The following mindfulness meditation is all about bringing your attention to the breath. It's a useful one to learn because you can do it anywhere at any time.

- Sitting comfortably, begin to breathe deeply - from the belly, not the chest, just as with the body scan meditation.
- Pay attention to the sensation as the breath moves in and out of your nostrils, and focus on that feeling. Feel the flow of breath in and out. Notice where you feel that breath in your body - in your belly, in your lower back, in your shoulder blades, and so on. Focus on one breath at a time.
- Continue to breathe in and out in this way for five minutes or so.
- If your mind is bombarding you with thoughts, gently redirect your thoughts back to your breath. If you're really struggling, you

could count a set number of seconds as you breathe in and out. For example, four seconds in and four seconds out.

Again, I highly recommend dipping into a meditation app to learn a wider selection of meditations. This helps to keep it fresh and interesting.

BUSTING MYTHS AND MISTAKES

The biggest mistake I see with meditation and mindfulness is just not giving it a try. Many people, my Rat Racer friend included, automatically think mindfulness and meditation is all airy fairy hippy stuff, or only for the more spiritual among us. I used to think the same thing before I gave it a try. I thought it was all a bit wishy-washy and not really for people like me - people who are focused on building success and wealth. But, because I believe in giving things a try, even if they're way out of my comfort zone, I decided to try it out.

Now I know that these techniques are a proven way to boost mental and physical health, improve concentration and performance, and generally move through life with more ease. These are practical techniques that should be right up there with other success-boosting attributes like communication, emotional intelligence and time management.

If you think about it, most of the time, the only thing that differentiates us in business is what's in our head. We're not athletes, so our physical strength or speed plays no role. Most of us aren't born into great wealth. I believe it's mindset that separates those who succeed from those who don't. For me, mindfulness and meditation are vital for attaining the right mindset for success.

Another common stumbling block is thinking you need loads of time for mindfulness or meditation. I hope this chapter and the simple mindfulness and meditation exercises included have dispelled that myth. Five minutes of mindful breathing does the world of good. But even if I don't have time for that, I'll take a mindful moment in the shower.

No, seriously. I jump in the shower as soon as I've turned it on, before the water has had a chance to warm up, and I imagine I'm jumping into a cold river in Holland, where my wife's from and where we have a little holiday cabin. I feel the cold water on my skin and how it immediately affects my breath. I feel alert and alive. And, as a bonus, it puts me, mentally, in that lovely calm and peaceful place where we've enjoyed so many happy family holidays. And then the water warms up and the moment is over. But it was a beautiful, mindful moment.

Even with my kids, I'll try and get them to tune into the here and now. To tune into their emotions. To be more mindful. To take a deep breath in a moment of frustration. It's working. My oldest daughter recently asked for a small water feature for her bedroom, so she could focus on the tinkling sound of water as she relaxed.

Even my Rat Racer friend next door, who thought meditation was hippy nonsense, was able to acknowledge the benefits of a mindful afternoon at the fishing lake. Those precious moments free of busyness and distraction served both of us well as we went home to finish building kitchen cabinets.

Arianna Huffington hit the nail on the head when she said meditation and mindfulness is not just another thing to 'do' in an already busy world. It's a necessity. As the old Zen saying goes, 'You should sit in meditation for 20 minutes a day, unless you're too busy, then you should sit for an hour!'

The busier we are, the more vital it is we take some time to find a bit of awareness, peace and clarity. If you're able to do this, you'll feel the benefits all day, not just for those blissful few minutes of awareness.

MEDITATION AND MINDFULNESS LESSONS FROM THE RAT RACER AND THE EXTRAORDINARY MILLIONAIRE

- The Rat Racer struggles to live in the present moment. They spend more time dwelling on the past or worrying about the future.

- The Extraordinary Millionaire knows that being aware of and enjoying the present is an important part of feeling at peace, especially in our busy, distracting world.
- The Rat Racer thinks mindfulness and meditation is only for those who are spiritual, religious or into airy fairy stuff.
- The Extraordinary Millionaire knows that mindfulness and meditation are evidence-based, practical, success-boosting techniques. Used together or separately, they help to calm the mind, promote feelings of positivity, reduce stress and anxiety, aid concentration, and more. Mindfulness and meditation help the Extraordinary Millionaire move through life with more ease.
- The Rat Racer thinks meditation is all sitting cross-legged and chanting.
- The Extraordinary Millionaire knows that there are many forms of meditation - some more spiritual than others. Mindfulness meditation, which simply involves bringing awareness to the body or breath, is ideal for anyone.
- The Rat Racer thinks their mind is too busy to meditate or be mindful.
- The Extraordinary Millionaire works at these techniques, building daily (or almost daily) routines of mindfulness and meditation. They'll also use a meditation app to help guide their practice and focus their awareness, even when their mind wants to wander.
- The Rat Racer thinks they don't have time for this. Their to-do list is long enough.
- The Extraordinary Millionaire knows that even just a brief minute of mindfulness or a mini meditation, or even just taking a few deep breaths, is powerful. This is not another thing to add to the to-do list. To meditate or be mindful is about doing nothing much at all, while you enjoy the present moment.

With its stress-busting effects, it's clear that mindfulness and meditation both have an effect on our physical wellbeing. Let's delve into that in more detail and see why physical wellness and sleep are an essential part of the Extraordinary Millionaire toolkit.

Chapter 6

Finding Time for Physical Wellness and Sleep in A Busy, Busy World

There was a time when my wife and I would have given almost anything for a good night's sleep. As parents of young children, we were regularly woken up by the kids in the night. And on top of that, my own night-time routine was terrible. I was going to bed too late, giving me six hours or so of shut-eye at best. I'd be looking at my phone and answering emails or doom-scrolling directly before going to bed (sometimes even in bed). Lying there, over-stimulated and wide awake, with busy thoughts running rampant through my head, it was no wonder I was having trouble dropping off. 'If I don't get to sleep right now,' I'd think to myself, 'I'm going to have less than five-and-a-half hours sleep.' Many nights, the countdown would get worse. 'Now I'm only going to get five hours,' I'd think. And so on.

It's not like there was a dramatic breaking point or anything. I just realised one day that it could all be so much better than this. That it was up to me to take better care of myself, and put in place strict routines to give myself the best chance of success, wealth and generally living a happier, more abundant life. I began to pay more attention to my sleep routine and my physical wellness.

Luckily, when it came to physical wellness, I had people around me who encouraged me to build good habits. My wife has always made time for the gym. And my Rat Racer friend next door was also a bit of a fitness nut.

LOOK AFTER YOUR BODY AND YOUR BODY WILL LOOK AFTER YOUR MIND

'It's weird,' I said to George. 'I can easily find time for a quick meditation in the morning, or spend a few minutes visualising my goals. But I really struggle to make time for exercise. I just can't seem to get excited about it or make it a priority in my day.'

I wasn't desperately unfit or unhealthy. But I knew I wasn't doing enough physical movement.

'What motivates you to do all that psychological stuff in the morning?' George asked. 'Because most people don't bother.'

It was a good question. I really thought about it before I answered him.

'Because I know it puts me in the best frame of mind for the day ahead. Because I feel calmer and more positive afterwards. And then I have a better day.'

'It's the same with exercise,' George said. 'My morning run and weekend cycle keep my stress levels down, give me more energy for the day, and - it sounds vain to say this but it's true - I feel better about myself physically. You know, it's like a self-esteem boost.'

I knew what he meant. I felt the same whenever I did make time to exercise.

'You're all about the positivity, right?' George said. 'Exercise means endorphins, and endorphins are the body's natural happy pills. Look after the body and the body looks after the mind.'

He was right, of course. Evidence shows that exercise is vital for physical and mental health, helping to reduce the risk of heart disease, diabetes, some cancers, depression, stress and even dementia. And yet knowing all that didn't really serve as a motivation for me - a guilt trigger, for sure, but not so much motivation to get out there and move more. George's advice to link it to my mental performance, positivity and success-building techniques certainly seemed more motivating.

But time was still an issue. This is where my wife's advice was invaluable. Despite having three young kids and running a business of her own, she *made* time for regular exercise. I really admired that.

'The way I see it,' she said. 'I can't help others if I don't help myself first. It's okay to put my wellbeing first for that hour while I'm at the gym because it helps me be there for everyone else who needs me. To be a better parent, partner, friend, and all that.'

This struck a chord. So many of my goals were about building this great, abundant life for my family. Passive income streams that would allow me the time and freedom to be more present with my family. That dream home with the woodland and zip wire where we could create amazing memories. Of course I wanted to be successful for myself (I've always been ambitious), but it was just as much about them.

How could I build the best life for my family, to show up for them in the best way possible, when I wasn't fully showing up for myself? When I wasn't looking after my physical wellbeing?

'You don't have to go to the gym,' my wife pointed out. 'I mean, I like it, but it's not really your thing, is it?'

She'd hit the nail on the head. I found the gym boring, plus all that extra time to travel there and back seemed like an additional barrier. (Some would say excuse, but . . .) If I had a home gym, I thought to myself, it'd be different, but at the time we were still in that little house. I needed to find something that worked for me in the here and now, not tell myself I'd get fit *one day* when we had all the kit at home.

'You just need to build more movement into the routines you already do and enjoy,' my wife said. 'Like walking further to get lunch or parking further away from the lake when you go fishing. Why don't you walk around the lake a few times before you sit down and fish?'

She was right. (She usually is.) The best way to be more active was to make it part of my everyday routine - and, wherever possible, do it outdoors. That was why I found the gym so boring. It was an indoor space with hardly any windows. No natural airflow or light. It felt stale to me. But being at the lake - being anywhere outdoors - was both calming and energising at the same time.

This led me to where I am now with exercise. I still could do more. I could always do better. But I make an effort to move more every day. Tying this into mindfulness and meditation has helped me, since that was already a part of my routine - indeed, an essential part of my routine. I'll often do a mindfulness meditation as I walk somewhere, focusing on my breath in and out, and the sensations in my body as I move. Or, if I want to do a little pre-meeting meditation to check in with how I'm feeling, instead of sitting still I might go for a quick stroll as I clear my mind and mentally prepare for the meeting ahead. It's not strictly meditation in the purist sense, since meditation usually requires you to do nothing except focus your awareness. Moving the body isn't typically part of the deal, but it certainly feels mindful and meditative to me - and very, very good for me.

With exercise, it was easy to pick up helpful habits from those around me. But sleep? As I delved deeper into the topic of sleep, I learned that most people I knew were also stuck in the same unhelpful night-time habits as I was. So I went on my own quest to learn more about sleep and unearth the tips and tools that would allow me to build a properly restful sleep routine.

THE POOR SLEEP EPIDEMIC

My Rat Racer friend and I were spending another afternoon at the fishing lake, and I'd mentioned that I was trying to get into a better sleep pattern.

'Sleep? I remember that,' George joked. 'To think I used to sleep in until whenever I wanted on a weekend. Now I'm lucky if the kids sleep in until 7am. At least I'm not the only one. Feels like everyone in the world is knackered these days. That's what most people say, isn't it? "I'm so TIRED."'

'But it's so bad for us,' I shook my head. 'Poor sleep is awful for physical and mental health. You know, I read that half of adults in the UK don't get enough sleep. How have we got to a state where everyone just accepts that it's okay to be tired all the time? That sleep is a luxury, not a necessity?'

'Dunno,' George said. 'But I can't see it changing anytime soon. Life's busy. And besides, sleep is for wimps, or so we're always being told by busy, busy, successful people. I'm surprised you're not one of those CEOs who bang on about how *little* sleep they need. The "I only need four hours a night" brigade. I wonder if they really do function well on four hours, or if it's just crap?'

'Actually, I think it is changing,' I said. 'I read this book *The Sleep Revolution* by Arianna Huffington all about the importance of sleep for success, productivity and performance. There's a bit of a pro-sleep movement among business leaders at the moment. People like Bill Gates and Jeff Bezos are saying sleep is vital to their success and makes them more productive. Google has nap pods in its offices. I think it's starting to change. People are starting to wake up to how dangerous sleep deprivation really is. Arianna Huffington describes it as "the new smoking."'

'That's a bit dramatic, isn't it?'

'Not according to the science. Not getting enough sleep is linked to all sorts. Increased risk of diabetes and obesity. High blood pressure. Weaker immune system. Depression. You know it can increase the risk of an early death by something like 12%?'

'Jesus!' George said. 'That can't be true, can it?'

As a fitness nut, someone who really prioritised staying in shape, I knew that would hit home for George.

'That's why she says it's the new smoking,' I said. 'Lack of sleep was even declared a public health problem in the US.'

George shook his head.

'The sad thing is,' I went on. 'A lot of people – especially people who are striving to be really successful – prioritise productivity over sleep. When the reality is productivity goes down when we're sleep deprived. Sleep more and you get more done. So those CEOs who proudly say they can get by on four hours a night? I don't know. If that's really true, good for them, but most of us need seven or eight hours sleep a night to function at our best. Good-quality sleep, that is.'

'God,' George sighed. 'What I wouldn't give for eight hours of unbroken sleep. Even when the kids don't wake us up, I find myself waking up for no reason.'

'No wonder. I've seen you popping up on Twitter and Facebook at 11pm,' I said.

'Yeah, but you only see that because you're on there too!'

He had me there.

'Not any more,' I said. 'I'm a new man. I've become evangelical about good sleep.'

'Oh yeah? Have you sent the kids off to boarding school then?' George joked.

'Hah. I may not be able to control being woken up by the kids, but there are plenty of things I can control. Like not taking my phone anywhere near the bedroom. Going to bed at the same time every night. That sort of stuff. The weird thing is, most of us already know the common-sense ways to have better sleep. We just don't do them. We neglect sleep, thinking it's fine to let it tumble down the list of priorities. Well, I'm done with all that.'

'It's as simple as that is it?' George asked. 'Staying off technology in the evenings and going to bed at the same time?'

'And getting up at the same time, even on weekends,' I added. 'There's a bit more to it than that, though. I've made some changes to our bedroom to make sleep easier. I've put in blackout curtains, and I got this cooling mat that goes under the bedsheet and keeps me cool at night. And I bought an actual alarm clock, so I'm not tempted to use my phone as an alarm. It's already working. And, we're doing the same thing with the kids, too - you know, no tablets in the evening, strict bedtime, blackout curtains, and so on. They're already sleeping better.'

'I like the sound of that,' George said. 'But I don't know about the no technology at night thing. That half an hour - alright, an hour - on my phone before going to sleep is the only time I have to myself to read the news or go on Twitter.'

'But is it really worth it?' I asked him. 'The blue light from the screen is telling your brain to be awake. And the news or whatever people are saying on Twitter is probably getting you riled up.'

'So what, I should just disengage from what's going on in the world?'

'Read a book!' I laughed. 'Remember them? Or a magazine or a newspaper. I've started reading real books again at night and I don't know why I ever gave it up in favour of scrolling or reading on my tablet. After reading something on actual paper, my brain is totally ready for sleep. It's not been stimulated by a lit-up screen. It's honestly making my sleep - and my days - so much better. It's life changing, just making that simple decision to prioritise my sleep.'

'Life changing?'

'100%. All that stuff I've been banging on about for years - the meditation, the goals, the law of attraction. Sleep was the missing ingredient in the pot.'

PRACTICAL WAYS TO LOOK AFTER THE BODY

Let's explore how you can put this into practice for yourself. Starting with looking after the body (and, in turn, the mind).

The overwhelming evidence tells us that we should all try to be more physically active. It's essential for living a healthy, happy and long life. A life that's full of abundance and fulfilment. According to the NHS, regular exercise can reduce the risk of early death by up to 30%. It's also essential for mental health and mental performance, since exercise is a proven way to boost concentration, memory and mood.

Finding time for regular exercise amidst the demands and pressures of a busy life is tough. I get that, and I've had my own struggles in that department. In my experience, the easiest way to move more is to just make it part of your everyday activities. For you, that might mean cycling to meet a friend instead of driving there, or parking a little further from the office so you can get more steps in. Taking the stairs instead of the lift. That sort of thing. Small, common-sense habits like this can really build up over time and contribute to a more active lifestyle.

It's also important to find activities that resonate with you. If you hate the gym, why force yourself to go there? Take up walking or jogging instead. Or wild swimming. Or badminton with a friend a couple of nights a week. Or get a dog.

You might also think back to the kind of sports you enjoyed when you were a child and seemingly had all the time in the world. How did you like to move then? Skipping, cycling, hula-hooping, roller-skating . . . there's no reason to give that up just because you're an adult. If you can find some sort of activity that you love, you'll be much more motivated to do it.

Me, I love fishing – a notoriously sit-down activity – so I turn that into a slightly more physical endeavour by walking a longer distance from the car to the lake, walking around the lake a few times to choose the best fishing spot, and just standing up and stretching more while I'm actually fishing. I try to do the same when I'm at work – move more, walk more, stand up more, stretch more. Little by little, I've become much more active than I used to be. Although there's always room for improvement.

How much exercise should you do? Government recommendations say at least 150 minutes a week, which is roughly 20 minutes a day. That's easy enough to achieve just by getting out for a lunchtime walk, although the recommendations are to do a variety of activities, if you can.

Exercise is, of course, only part of the puzzle. What we put into our body matters. You can be a super-fit person who runs five miles a day, but if you only ever eat ultra-processed junk, you're hardly giving your body the best chance.

I'm not going to tell you what you should and shouldn't eat. To eat well is to eat without restriction or guilt – it's to eat a little of whatever you fancy, and to make sure you're getting a variety of foods across the course of a week. As Michael Pollan, author of *In Defense of Food* so neatly put it, 'Eat food. Not too much. Mostly Plants.'

If you're wondering why I mention food and exercise in a book that's about tools for success and wealth, it's because these *are* tools for success and wealth. I can't show up and perform my best at work if I'm not taking the best possible care of myself. Besides, it makes me a better partner, father, boss and colleague – by helping myself, I'm better able to help others. And that makes me happier, which in turn boosts my mental health, and the positive cycle continues.

BUILDING A SLEEP-FRIENDLY ROUTINE

Likewise, sleep is a vital tool for success. On the surface, the effects of good sleep habits are not so easy to quantify in terms of business achievements (I've never heard anyone say 'Oh, I closed that deal because I slept well,' for instance), but it's certainly true that we perform better, and therefore have the best chance of success, when we're well rested. I know I do.

There's a wealth of scientific evidence proving that sleep has a significant effect on our mental and physical capabilities and health. Experiments have shown that people who are deprived of sleep develop increasingly severe problems, including progressive degeneration in perception, concentration and other cognitive functions. In a business context, that translates into sub-par performance and poor decision making - which is exactly what you *don't* want when you're trying to enhance your success and grow your wealth.

Quite simply, you get less done when you're tired. A study by global think tank Rand showed that the UK economy loses £40 billion a year through sleep-related absenteeism and 'presenteeism' (where people turn up for work but perform poorly because they're tired). The study also found that those who sleep fewer than six hours per night lose more working days each year than those who sleep more.

Why are we getting sleep so wrong? Technology - or, more specifically, the increasing need to be connected and available all the time - has a lot to answer for. Smartphones especially have made it difficult to switch off when we're away from work, and it's not uncommon for people to be answering emails or on social media at 11pm. One Deloitte study even found that a shocking one third of Brits check their smartphone in the middle of the night. In the middle of the night!

The light emitted from phones and tablets is blue light, which has been proven to supress melatonin (which is essential for good health and helps fight obesity). Blue light tells our brains to be active and awake, and that's why looking at a screen directly before bed or during the night is so bad for sleep. Research has shown that people who read on their tablet at night have poor-quality sleep and wake up feeling more tired than those who read a physical book. That's why I now read either a physical book in bed, or I dig out my old-school Kindle, which doesn't have a lit-up screen.

Good sleep, then, starts before you even put your head on the pillow. My wind-down routine starts one hour before I go to bed and is designed to calm my brain so I can drop off easily. This hour is a strict 'no screen' time, meaning no phones or tablets. TVs also emit blue light, but it doesn't seem to keep me as awake as looking at my phone screen, so I find I can leave the telly on until around 15 minutes before I head up to bed and still drop off easily. If the TV is too much of a stimulus for you (say, if you find yourself shouting at the evening news), then definitely include that in your 'no screen' hour. It's also not a great idea to have a TV in your bedroom. (It's tempting to stay up later if you're watching TV in bed, and it reduces the chance of doing other calming activities, like reading.)

My night-time routine also includes having a calming herbal tea at the start of my 'no screen' hour - any later than that and you may find your bladder waking you up in the night! Others swear by hot milk as a soothing night-time drink. We all know we shouldn't drink caffeine in the evening, even regular tea, but there are plenty of other drinks and food that can mess with your sleep, such as alcohol and spicy or fatty foods. And you know the old saying about cheese giving you weird dreams? It's based on scientific fact; cheese contains amino acid tyramine, which has been shown to make the brain feel more awake. So, instead of drinking a nice glass of red wine and tucking into a bit of brie before bed, what you should do - if you're peckish, that is - is eat a banana. Bananas contain magnesium, which is good for relaxing the muscles, as well as melatonin and serotonin, both of which aid sleep.

On those evenings when I'm feeling particularly stressed, or I'm feeling really alert and awake and therefore might struggle to nod off, I turn to meditation. Just five minutes of meditation before bed can help me wind down.

When I'm in bed, I also find it helpful to spend just a few minutes - literally, just two or three minutes - reviewing my day, thinking about went well and what I'm grateful for from the day. I may even use some positive affirmations or visualisation techniques. I find that, rather than keeping my mind active and busy, this actually helps clear my brain. Then, I'll pick up whatever book I'm into and read for a little while. Generally, thanks to my wind-down routine, it's not long before my eyelids start to feel heavy.

Now for the age-old question. How much sleep do you really need? Everyone's ideal amount of sleep is different, so maybe those CEOs claiming they do fine on four hours a night are telling the truth (but I doubt it). The National Sleep Foundation recommends adults get seven to nine hours of sleep a night, but you should do what works for you. If you feel like you've overslept when you have anything more than seven hours, then seven hours is probably the ideal amount for you. You may prefer nine or ten hours. It doesn't matter so much what your magic number is, what matters more is that you stick to that number and make it a part of your routine.

Personally, I need eight hours and that's what I aim for every night – regardless of what's going on and how busy I am. And because routine is so important, I stick to the same amount of sleep on weekends too, rather than sleeping in for an extra couple of hours. For the most part, then, I go to bed and get up at roughly the same time, even on weekends.

Knowing what time I need to get up in the morning, and knowing that I need eight hours of sleep, it's easy to work out what time I need to go to sleep each night, and what time to start my wind-down hour.

And on the rare occasion when I do wake up in the night, I get up and go downstairs, make myself a drink and eat a banana. I might do a brief meditation as well. Then I leave it five or ten minutes before going back to bed. Whatever you do, don't reach for your phone or the TV remote.

A good morning routine is another important part of sleep management. Rather than snoozing the alarm over and over again, then rushing around like a mad thing, it's important to give yourself plenty of time in the morning to do all the things you need to, including having breakfast, and, wherever possible, having a little time to yourself (for meditation, visualisation, exercise, or whatever you like). This will help you feel more organised and prepared for the day ahead, as well as more awake and refreshed - as opposed to tumbling out of bed and into the car 15 minutes later.

This night-time and morning routine hasn't just given my performance and wellbeing a boost - it's helped my whole family too. My wife and I have got our kids into the same routine (no screens before bed, etc.) as we believe it's important to set them up with good sleep behaviours that they can continue as adults.

GIVE YOUR BEDROOM A SLEEP-FRIENDLY MAKEOVER

Aside from routine, environment has a huge impact on how well I sleep - specifically light levels, temperature and noise. We all know this but most of us neglect to do anything about it. I know I neglected it.

Firstly, humans need darkness to be able to sleep properly. It's obvious, yet lots of us have bedrooms with curtains that let in light, or lit-up alarm clocks and smartphones right next to our bed. All these things need to go. Invest in good-quality blackout curtains or blinds and you'll never look back. I didn't realise until I got blackout blinds how much the early-morning sunlight in summer disturbed my sleep. I was losing easily a couple of hours' good-quality sleep every night. Now, not even a sliver of light gets into our room - it's pitch black - and it has transformed how well we sleep.

Temperature is just as important. Most research agrees that the optimum temperature for sleep is between 15°C and 19°C. Anything over 23°C or below 12°C is generally considered to be disruptive to sleep. Nowadays, for those warmer months, I have air conditioning in my bedroom, which may seem like an extravagance in our British climate, but I think of it as an investment in my own performance. If you don't like air conditioning, or it's not viable for you, I recommend the ChiliPad mat - but more on that coming up.

While you can control the light and temperature in your bedroom, you probably have less control over noise. If you live in a busy area, or in a flat with noisy neighbours, this will undoubtedly affect your sleep. Thick blinds and curtains will help keep out some of the noise, but it's also worth keeping a set of earplugs next to the bed. We're lucky in that our house is quiet at night, so I mainly use the earplugs when my daughter has a sleepover with her friends. They also come in very handy whenever I'm staying in a hotel.

And if possible, invest in a good bed, mattress and pillows. You spend a third of your life in bed, so you should at least be comfortable there. Your mattress in particular isn't something you should 'make do' with. Also, be sure to turn the mattress every three months, replace the mattress every five to ten years, and replace the pillows every two years. You can also tailor your pillows by having thinner pillows if you sleep on your front and deeper pillows if you sleep on your back. Seriously, it's time to start paying attention to these things.

MAKE TECHNOLOGY YOUR FRIEND

There are lots of tools and products out there that promise to help you have healthier, happier days and more restful nights. Here are some that have actually worked for me.

For physical fitness, it's worth investing in a smart watch or fitness tracking band - if only to keep an eye on the number of steps you do each day. Trust me, if you're at all a competitive person, being aware of those numbers will help you move more.

For sleep, I highly recommend the Headspace meditation app. It includes lots of helpful guided meditations that are designed to promote sleep. There's also a brilliant sleep improvement app called Sleepio, which uses evidence-based cognitive behavioural therapy techniques and lets you design a sleep improvement course that's tailored to you.

Another product that I love is the Withings Aura sleep system and monitor. This suite of tools includes the 'Aura' - an alarm clock that sits next to your bed - as well as an accompanying app and a sleep-tracking sensor pad that you put under your sheet or mattress. The sensor monitors your sleep by measuring things like your movement and heartrate during the night. The accompanying app will show you when you woke up, spikes of activity, and overall quality of your sleep. Best of all, because it's monitoring how well you're sleeping, it can wake you up at the optimum time in your sleep cycle.

Normal alarm clocks go off at a set time, and if you happen to be in a deep sleep state at that time, it can feel like you're being bashed over the head. The Aura, however, knows whether you're in a light or deep sleep state, and you can set it to wake you up within a certain window, depending on what stage of sleep you're in. Say, for example, you usually get up at 7am. You can set the Aura to wake you 30 minutes either side of that time, when you're in the optimum stage for waking. So, if you start to come into a lighter sleep mode at 6.40am, the sensor detects this and the Aura begins to wake you up. It also wakes you very softly and gradually, starting with a faint blue light (which we know signals the brain to be more active) that gradually fills the room. Then it starts to play soft music. I can't stress enough how lovely it is to wake up in this gentle, natural way rather than bolting up and bashing at an alarm clock - or worse, reaching for my phone and seeing tons of notifications first thing.

Speaking of light, the light that's most conducive to sleep is, surprisingly, red light. The Aura also has a mode for helping you get to sleep that uses red light and soothing music. Gradually, the red light and music fades until you are left with a completely dark, silent room.

And when it comes to keeping cool, I really like the ChiliPad, which is kind of like an electric blanket but it can keep you cool as well as warm. The pad - which goes under the sheets, but don't worry, you can't tell it's there - circulates cool water through the night, keeping your body cool. It can also circulate warm water to keep you cosy in the winter.

Thanks to these tools - and having a good exercise and sleep routine - I'm now more active and I get the right amount of high-quality sleep each night. I have better mornings. I perform better and am more productive throughout the day. That's why exercise and sleep management are two of my biggest tips for those who want to boost their performance. And the great news is that, for most people, these are relatively simple things to achieve. With a few changes to your routine, environment and, importantly, your attitude, you can move more, sleep better, feel better and be more productive. Every day.

SLEEP AND WELLBEING LESSONS FROM THE RAT RACER AND THE EXTRAORDINARY MILLIONAIRE

- Someone who's stuck in the Rat Racer culture may struggle to find time for physical activity, or finds that it constantly gets shoved to the bottom of the priority list.
- The Extraordinary Millionaire knows that, in order to take care of others and be the best they can be, they must take care of themselves.
- Even if they do take care of their physical body, the Rat Racer doesn't necessarily connect that to the importance of good sleep. After all, everyone is tired, aren't they? It's part and parcel of modern life.
- The Extraordinary Millionaire knows that sleep has a huge impact on physical and mental performance, as well as physical and mental health.
- The Rat Racer's bedtime routine generally involves doom-scrolling social media, answering emails or reading the news on their phone directly before going to sleep. Then they lie there, wide awake, frustrated that they can't sleep.
- The Extraordinary Millionaire has a strict wind-down, 'no-screen' period every night before bed. They'll also use calming techniques like meditation and visualisation. And when they want to read, they pick up a physical book or magazine, or an old fashioned Kindle without a backlit screen.
- The Rat Racer doesn't have a set bedtime - not even a rough one. Their bedtime is all over the place, especially on weekends.
- The Extraordinary Millionaire knows that routine is key, so they generally go to bed and get up at roughly the same time every day.

- Exhausted, the Rat Racer snoozes their alarm for as long as they can get away with in the morning. (And, of course, their alarm is their smartphone.) Then they rush around and barely have time for important morning activities, like exercising, or eating a nourishing breakfast.
- The Extraordinary Millionaire leaves the phone downstairs and uses an alarm clock to wake up. They make time in the mornings for all the things that set them up for a successful day.
- The Rat Racer knows that environment is important for a good night's sleep but hasn't got around to making changes to their bedroom.
- The Extraordinary Millionaire invests in a sleep-friendly bedroom, including blackout curtains, cooling technology, and a quality mattress and pillows.

I really had to go on a learning journey to improve my sleep - working hard to unlearn bad habits and learn better ones. Which brings us to the next technique in the Extraordinary Millionaire toolkit: embracing lifelong learning.

Chapter 7

Becoming A Lifelong Learner

'This year, I'm going for it,' my Rat Racer friend said. 'I'm going to start my business. Start working for myself instead, finally. Doing more of what makes me happy.'

It was early January and the neighbour and I - as people so often do in January - got onto the topic of resolutions.

'The cycling app?' I asked.

He nodded.

'Good for you. So what's the first step?'

'Well, there are loads of tech businesses in Reading, and it's only up the road. So I thought I'd start by joining a few networking groups in that area. I've been away from the frontline for a little while, and I could do with beefing up my contacts a bit.'

By this point, George had advanced beyond his tech sales position and was now in more of a middle-management role. He was on a good leadership track, but it was becoming increasingly clear that it just wasn't what he wanted to do for the rest of his life. And with the promotion, came more stress and more demands on his time. He was tired. He'd let his hobbies and interests slide. He wore the unmistakable expression of someone who was stuck in a rut.

'I just get the feeling that it's now or never for me,' he said. 'If I don't give this a shot now, I never will.'

I knew what he meant. I'd experienced the same urgency more than a decade earlier when I quit my own comfortable job to start a career in property.

'You won't regret it,' I said.

'Yeah, but there's so much to do and learn. Actually, I was hoping to maybe raid your bookshelves . . .'

Lucky for George, the bloke next door - that's me - had an overflowing collection of business and entrepreneurship books to inspire and educate.

This sudden interest in my book collection was a good sign. I knew from experience that becoming a successful entrepreneur is all about personal development and continual education - both in terms of business skills and mindset skills. If he was willing to learn - to make himself vulnerable and admit how much he *didn't* yet know - George's hopes of escaping the rat race stood a much better chance.

I grinned. 'Borrow away!'

SOAKING UP ADVICE AND INSPIRATION FROM SUCCESSFUL PEOPLE

'Huh, you don't have as many property books as I expected,' George was glancing along my bookshelves.

I did read books by my property peers, but George was right, my collection of non-fiction books went way beyond property, and leaned heavily towards autobiographies of successful people, books about mindset techniques, practical how-to business and investment books, and more. In short, it spanned everything from the very niche strategy books to generic 'Here's how I made it big' books.

'Have you really read all of these?' he asked.

'I must've read pretty much every major entrepreneurship book out there.'

'But you can't possibly remember all this stuff. It's information overload.'

'I don't have to remember every little thing they say. Some of these books just motivate me and spur me on to do better, because I'm inspired by their success story. Others reinforce the feeling that I'm on the right track - as in, I'm already doing a lot of the things they talk about, so it reassures me that I'm going in the right direction, which is motivating in itself. And other books, I might only get a single gem from them. One amazing nugget of information or a tip that stays with me forever. Even that one little nugget makes the whole book worth it.'

He pulled Richard Branson's autobiography off the shelf and started flipping through it. 'So if I read this, it'll help me become an entrepreneur, even though it's got nothing to do with tech businesses.'

'I mean, by all means read as many books by tech entrepreneurs as you can get your hands on, because that's your field of interest. But you don't just have to learn from people in your field. There's so much to learn from any successful person. How they got started. Their habits and traits. How they spend their time. What's important to them, and so on. Just soak it all in. That's my biggest tip when you're getting started - seek out other successful people and learn as much as you can from them.'

'It's not all about books, though,' I went on. 'There are podcasts, TED talks, industry forums, all that stuff. I've been spending a lot of time lately watching this guy on YouTube. He's got tons of followers and every video he makes goes viral. But he doesn't just go viral because he's got lots of followers - he understands the algorithm. He makes great content, knows how to tell a story. And he knows how to optimise that content with descriptions and hashtags. By watching what this guy does, I'm learning how to use YouTube to promote my business.'

'What about a business mentor?' George asked.

'I have a life coach as a mentor,' I said. 'She's taught me lots of the mindset techniques that I'm always going on about. Positive affirmations, visualisation, all that stuff. She coaches me on my mental health and performance, reminds me of the mindset tools I have at my disposal, and helps me refocus on my goals. And if I have any issues - like, if I'm feeling unmotivated or a bit directionless - she helps me unpack that and find a positive way forward. It's been brilliant.'

'Sounds more like a therapist,' George said.

'Well, I guess good coaching is kind of therapeutic. I always come away from a session feeling calmer and more positive.'

'But you haven't had a business mentor . . .?'

'No, I never had a property or business mentor when I was getting started. Although I would have loved to. It was a lot harder to get started then. There were books and some property investing courses - although some of them were just rip-offs. Now there's so much choice for people to learn about property. It's far more accessible. I learnt by doing. Having a life coach helped me build the mental tools for success, while I learned the practical property and investing strategies as I went along. I'm still learning, of course. If you have the chance to work with a mentor, or a life coach, go for it. But you can learn from all sorts of people - doesn't have to be a formal mentorship or coaching relationship.'

'Are you offering to share your infinite wisdom with me?' George smiled.

'Hah, that wasn't what I was getting at, but of course. I'm here for whatever you need. Pep talks. Someone to listen. A second opinion. Practical help. Whatever. What I was going to say is you can learn from anyone you admire, whether or not they're a mentor. I have contractors and employees who are experts in their field - on everything from marketing to planning laws - and I'm always learning from them.'

'This is your day job, though,' George said. 'I'm going to have to start my business as a side gig, and do all this alongside working full-time.' He sighed. 'It's a bit overwhelming if I'm honest. It's hard to know where to start.'

'But you don't have to do everything all at once. Think of it like a funnel.'

STARTING BROAD AND NARROWING DOWN

'A funnel?' George asked.

'Yeah,' I said, 'as in, it's widest at the top, and it narrows down at the base as you get more discerning. I started by funnelling in all the masses of free content I could get my hands on. Forums, online groups, YouTube vids, websites, free ebooks and downloads, checklists and resources, networking meetings, property exhibitions, all those free resources out there. That's the stuff that's easy to access. It doesn't require any financial outlay, so it's a fairly low-stakes, easy way to immerse yourself in whatever you're learning about - in my case, property and investing.

I just immersed myself in the industry. At this point, all you're spending is your own time.'

'Right . . .' George said.

'Next, I started making a financial investment in my education. Starting with books. They're not expensive, but it's still something of an investment. Then you begin to narrow down even more as your expertise and knowledge begins to grow. You might want to invest in some courses - or qualifications, or maybe even paid mentorship programmes. It's a bigger financial commitment, but you're doing less of it than you were at the top of the funnel, where you're learning from everything you can get your hands on. As you move down the funnel, you get choosier about your learning resources because the stakes are greater. You're making a bigger investment.'

'What you mean is, don't pay for questionable courses?'

'Exactly. Especially in the wealth creation industry, there are plenty of disreputable operators out there who'll sell you a course for thousands of pounds, then you find out it doesn't contain any real substance. You need to do your due diligence on the people and resources you choose to learn from. Their qualifications, track record, what exactly you get for your money, etc. Just do your research.'

'But for now I start at the top of the funnel . . .' George said, eyeing up the book in his hand.

'Right. Start with the free and inexpensive resources that are easily accessible and then build on that.'

LEARNING HOW TO LEARN

'Oh, here's another good one for you,' I said, digging a book out from the shelf.

'Limitless,' George read the front cover. 'Upgrade your brain, learn anything faster . . . it's brain training stuff?'

'Brain training, memory . . . Basically it's learning *how* to learn, how to make the brain more efficient so you can retain more information. Seriously, this guy, Jim Kwik, is brilliant. He did another book, Super Brain. He's got a podcast too, and courses. You should check him out. Or other brain training techniques, if you prefer. These techniques will have you looking like a genius.'

'How's that?'

'Did I ever tell you I can recite Pi to 200 digits?'

George snorted, 'You're joking?'

I started reciting the numbers. '3.1415926535 8979323846 2643383279 . . .'

After a minute, George stopped me.

'Okay, cool trick, but I don't see what learning Pi has got to do with me becoming an entrepreneur.'

'It doesn't have to be Pi. Could be anything that you struggle with or want to improve. Like remembering people's names. Or just improving your memory in general. Get your brain working more effectively and you'll be in a better position to retain all this . . .' I gestured at the stacks of books in my office.

'It's just about learning how to learn,' I continued. 'So you can hold more info. If you're going to go on a learning journey, learning how to learn is a good first step.'

YOUR PERSONAL LEARNING JOURNEY

If there's one chapter in this book that's the most important - the one secret ingredient that will help you unlock all the other tools in the Extraordinary Millionaire toolkit, it's this one: becoming a lifelong learner. If you're going to become successful, grow your wealth and create an extraordinarily abundant life, you have to become an information sponge. And your learning journey doesn't end when you eventually become successful. Far from it. I'm still learning all the time - how to be a better leader, new property trends and strategies, how to better market my business, building my personal brand, branching out into presenting and education . . .

You'll never be 'done' as a learner. Not if you really want to become successful. That's why this chapter is called 'Becoming a *lifelong* learner.' Emphasis on the lifelong.

'Continuous learning is the minimum requirement for success in any field,' said author and motivational speaker Brian Tracy (the guy who wrote the legendary self-help book *Eat That Frog*). You'll probably have gathered by now that I'm a business and entrepreneurship book junkie. I can't get enough of them, and I'll read anything I can get my hands on – anything from selling to meditation. If I think it'll help me become more successful, I'll read it.

One thing all these different books have in common is an emphasis on continual improvement. 'Never stop learning' has become something of a motto of mine, and I believe it's been a critical element of my success. Hands down, the best thing you can do is invest (time, energy and money) in your own continuing education. In my view, continual learning is what differentiates the wannabes from the super-successful.

In other words, never fall into the trap of thinking you know it all. If you want to succeed and stay at the top of your game, you'll need to keep learning new things. Likewise, don't fall into the trap of thinking that, just because you can't (yet) do something, or don't (yet) know how to do something, that you'll never be able to do it. This is the difference between the *growth mindset* (believing that anything can be learned and improved with time and effort) and the *fixed mindset* (believing that skills and qualities are inherent or inbuilt). I talk more about this in Chapter 14.

Clearly I'm passionate about education – my own, obviously, but also helping others learn (whether it's property investment strategies, or the mindset tools for success). That's why I'm sitting here writing this book. I wanted to distil the proven strategies and techniques that I've learned over the years and that have helped me build an abundant life. It's also why I run a property mentorship programme for aspiring property investors and developers. I would have loved to have access to such a programme when I was starting out and now I get to offer that to others.

So what are the best ways to become a lifelong, continual learner? As a property investor, I learnt a lot simply by doing, starting small, getting better at various property strategies, and then tackling bigger and bigger projects. So, I went from renting out a spare room in my first home, to me moving out and turning the whole house into an HMO (where the bedrooms are rented individually to tenants, instead of renting the whole house on one contract). Then, once I'd got a few successful HMOs under my belt, I started developing properties with the intention of converting them into HMOs. Then I began to tackle bigger developments - converting office blocks into apartments, and so on.

You learn so much by doing, learning all the time from what went well and what could be improved next time. So one of my biggest tips is to not let a fear of failure hold you back from doing whatever it is you want to do. You probably won't be an overnight success (although, hey, maybe you will). But you will learn and get better over time, just as I did. Don't be afraid of failure, basically - but more on that in Chapter 14.

Of course, you need to supplement this with more traditional education - learning by learning, as well as learning by doing! Let's explore some of my favourite ways of learning.

TAPPING INTO A RICH VARIETY OF EDUCATION SOURCES

Remember how I described learning as being like a funnel? You have a mass of free, easily accessible resources at the top of the funnel, then you begin to narrow down to paid-for content, from the inexpensive to the bigger investments.

Bottom line, there are many, many ways you can learn. At the top of the funnel, depending on your chosen field, you might tap into:

- **Forums and social media groups.** Sites like propertyforum.com (which I own - other forums are available) provide a wealth of free information, and act as a good way to keep up with trends. Whatever your chosen field, I bet there are forums, Facebook and LinkedIn groups out there to help you connect with advice and info.
- **Relevant individuals on social media.** One of the great things about social media is it gives you access to those people who are leading the life you seek to lead. Be sure to follow individual experts in your chosen field, and seek out other inspirational figures on social media. Soak up every bit of advice and inspiration they put out there. Some experts also do informal 'live' sessions on platforms like Instagram, or publish free articles on LinkedIn.
- **Blogs, newsletters and podcasts.** Obviously seek out those that are relevant to your particular industry, but don't overlook the value of more general resources. Jim Kwik's podcast, Kwik Brain, for example, may not be obviously relevant to your field, but it'll help you learn and retain information in a more efficient way.
- **Seminars and events.** Depending on your industry, there are probably free seminars, shows and exhibitions that you can attend. In property, for instance, there are numerous annual property exhibitions and I found these were great for immersing myself in the industry and expanding my network. There are also property investment companies and larger property developers that hold free seminars, online and offline. (True, the goal of these seminars is usually to sell you products and investments, so always do your own homework after the seminar and never buy anything on the day. But they can be a good way of learning about specific strategies and what's going on in the market.)
- **Educational videos on YouTube.** Think YouTube is all music videos and people doing daft things? Think again. I've learned a lot from YouTube over the years, and you'll find lots of quality content on there covering everything from digital marketing, to personal branding, to investing strategies, and more.

When it comes to paying for content, especially books, I recommend:

- **Reading as many books as you can about your chosen investment strategies and/or industry.** I get that it can be difficult to find time and space for reading, but it's on you to carve out gaps wherever you can - remember, this is about investing in your future. As a busy dad of three, I might get up a bit earlier in the morning so I can have 15 minutes of quiet reading time before the kids get up. I'll also read at night and listen to audiobooks as I'm driving in the car.
- **Delving into more general business, autobiographies, self-help and entrepreneurship books.** I'm always inspired by other people's journeys and intrigued by their personal formula for success, which is why I love autobiographies of successful people. (For one thing, you'll be surprised how many traits successful people have in common, and the more you read these sorts of books, the more you can recognise and emulate those traits.) I've also found some of the more 'self-helpy' books about mindfulness, meditation, goal setting and so on to be really valuable, as they've given me practical tools for getting the most out of my time and energy.

And as for courses, you can:

- **Head to the big learning platforms.** Whatever you want to learn - whether it's email marketing, property development, coding or whatever, I'll bet the big learning platforms have a course for you. Udemy is a valuable resource for online courses (full disclosure, I've created a course for Udemy in the past), but there are plenty of other online learning platforms out there, such as Coursera and LearnDirect.
- **Seek out specific courses from people and organisations you admire.** I'm currently creating a suite of property-related courses, and you'll find that more and more leaders in the business/entrepreneurship/ investing space are offering their own courses, outside of the big learning platforms. But just as I said to my Rat Racer neighbour, please, please do your due diligence before you fork over your hard-earned money.

A quick word on that due diligence point. There are a lot of dodgy operators out there who will have you believing you can become a millionaire in six months, if you only sign up for their expensive course. Beware of get-rich-quick promises. There are no shortcuts, trust me. Becoming successful, growing your wealth, building an amazing life . . . it takes hard work and commitment. It's 100% worth it, but it's not an overnight journey, and don't let anyone tell you otherwise.

With this in mind, always do your due diligence on people who are offering courses or paid-for mentorship programmes. Ask yourself:

- What is this educator's track record in their field of expertise? If it's not immediately obvious, don't be afraid to ask for proof of their track record.
- Where relevant, what are their qualifications?
- What support and resources will you get for your money? For example, will you get one-on-one time, or will you just have a load of content dumped on you?
- What are their reviews like? What do past attendees of this course have to say?

LEARNING FROM OTHER SUCCESSFUL PEOPLE

Your goal is to learn from others who have become successful. Books are a great way to do this. But so is mentorship. It goes without saying that buddying up with a more experienced person in your field is a brilliant way to learn. That goes for property investing, or any other form of business. Mentorship can come in all shapes and sizes, from a formal learning relationship to something altogether looser and more relaxed. It can be as simple as an occasional coffee and chat with someone you admire, or as structured as weekly sessions that follow a set agenda. It may not even be focused on your area of business – you can learn a great deal from someone who has, for example, built a successful business in a different field, or juggled the demands of entrepreneurship and parenthood, or built a wildly successful personal brand online . . .

There are also paid mentorship programmes out there, and these can be a great option as you begin to work your way down that learning funnel. Why pay for mentorship? Because it can offer you much greater one-on-one access to your mentor, and their network. With my mentorship programme, for example, I work with budding property investors to identify a good strategy for them and find potential property deals - plus, depending on their needs, I can also connect them with my team of project managers, planning consultants, architects and so on. I can even oversee the development with them.

But again, if you're going down a paid mentorship route, always do your due diligence on the person you'll be working with.

Also remember that you can learn from anyone, regardless of whether or not it's a formal mentorship relationship. Like how, when I wanted to learn about making YouTube videos, I identified one of the most successful YouTubers on the platform and devoured all his content. I learned what makes a good YouTube video by looking at his most popular videos. Likewise, I also learn from the people in my team. I learn from architects and project managers and marketers and estate agents all the time.

Basically, try to recognise the gaps in your knowledge and begin to fill in those gaps by learning from the people around you.

And as your experience and success grows, make sure you pay it forward - by which I mean be willing to connect with those less experienced than you, share your nuggets of wisdom, and help them on their own journey to becoming an Extraordinary Millionaire.

NETWORKING YOUR WAY TO SUCCESS

If you're serious about becoming a successful entrepreneur or investor - especially if you're focusing on property investing - you'd better get serious about networking. In particular, networking groups, both offline and online, are a really useful way to grow your personal network, find the experts you need (maybe even a mentor), and learn from others.

Personally, I don't go in for those general networking groups, where you sit in a stuffy meeting room, drinking bad coffee, listening to a load of people plug their businesses. That's just my opinion. You may want to check out some of these general business networking groups in your local area to see if they provide any value for you.

I've certainly gained a lot of value from property-specific networking groups, and I recommend you seek out more specific networking opportunities that are relevant to your field.

These networking opportunities may be in-person, if you're close to somewhere like London. But in-person opportunities aside, don't overlook the value of online networking, via forums and social media. After all, there are no geographical boundaries online, so you can connect with all sorts of people and get a feel for what they're investing in, how they're growing their business, and so on. Useful places to start are LinkedIn, Facebook, Reddit and industry forums, like the Property Forum.

STICKING AT IT

A few months after raiding my bookshelves, I asked the Rat Racer how his continual education journey was going, and the honest answer was 'not great'. He'd read a few borrowed books, been to a few networking meetings, but that was about it. And he was frustrated that he was struggling to get going.

My response was, 'Of course you're struggling to get going. You don't know enough yet!'

My Rat Racer friend was still circling around the rim of the funnel. He hadn't invested a single pound in his education. He hadn't developed that voracious appetite for learning. What he wanted was an easy, quick path to building a successful business. No such thing exists.

I see a lot of people fall at the early hurdles and fail to escape the rat race. And a lot of the time it's because they haven't committed themselves fully to this continual education journey. They weren't willing to become a student of their chosen industry. I get it. It's hard to find time for this. But find time you must, if you want to really succeed. Try to see it for what it really is - an investment in your (and your loved ones') future.

Also, learn to accept the fact that you'll never arrive at a point at which you master everything there is to master. You will have to maintain that appetite for learning. But this is a good thing. Wouldn't it be boring if you knew everything? I relish the ever-changing nature of the property markets and being my own boss. I love the fact that there are new investment strategies to explore, new self-help techniques to incorporate into my toolbox, and so on.

If you too can embrace this notion of being constantly curious - constantly on the lookout for new learning opportunities - you'll be giving yourself the very best chance of success.

CONTINUAL LEARNING LESSONS FROM THE RAT RACER AND THE EXTRAORDINARY MILLIONAIRE

- Someone with a Rat Racer mindset may get too comfortable in their knowledge or even fall into the trap of thinking they know everything there is to know.
- Someone with an Extraordinary Millionaire mindset knows that they will never be 'done' with learning. There will always be new things to learn, even when they become enormously successful.
- The Rat Racer may happily learn from free content - which is great - but they struggle to progress beyond that and deepen their learning. They don't see their continual education as a financial investment, and this is a huge mistake.
- The Extraordinary Millionaire knows that continual education is one of the most important investments they'll ever make. And not just a financial investment but also an investment of their time and energy.
- The Rat Racer doesn't carve out time for their continual learning, then gets frustrated that they've stagnated.

- The Extraordinary Millionaire makes time for learning. They make learning a part of everyday life – listening to audiobooks and podcasts on the way to work, for example.

I've talked a lot about making time for these techniques amidst the everyday pressures and demands of a busy life. So let's dwell a little on that subject and look at how you can build a regular routine that sets you up for success.

Chapter 8

Building A Regular Routine of Success-Boosting Habits

Moving house is never exactly fun, but this move was one of the most satisfying days of my life. After so many years picturing this perfect family home, we were finally moving in.

This house had everything we'd ever dreamed of: plenty of space for our growing family, peace and quiet, eight acres of private woodland in an area of outstanding natural beauty. It was perfect for camp fires, quality family time and, yes, building a zip line. Just like the one I'd had when I was a child. Needless to say, we fell in love with this house instantly.

As soon as we were settled, we had our old neighbours over for a family barbecue.

'Come see the yurt,' I said to George.

In our previous house, my office was a small-ish spare room. It was fine - I was certainly grateful to have that space - but it wasn't the most inspiring place to spend time. Part of wanting a house with more outdoor space was creating an outdoor office. Somewhere I could physically 'go' to work, and leave behind at the end of the day. And because I like things a bit different, I chose a yurt, complete with wood-burning stove, carpets and comfy sofas. It's a yurt that any Mongolian nomadic family would be proud of!

'Blimey,' George said, taking it all in. 'You've well and truly left the rat race behind, haven't you? You're someone who works in a yurt.'

I suspect up until this point, George had thought I was just dabbling in property. That one day I'd go back to having a 'proper' job. He knew my property business was going pretty well - after all, I'd managed to keep a roof over my family's heads - but he had no idea it had grown into a multi-million-pound portfolio. Visiting the new house, it was obvious that I'd been seriously growing my wealth over the years.

'I'm impressed,' he said.

'It's pretty great,' I acknowledged. 'I love it here. So, how are the new neighbours?'

As an added bonus, we had managed to retain our old house as a rental property, and the tenants had just moved in.

'They seem alright,' George replied. 'Pretty quiet.'

George, too, was uncharacteristically quiet as he looked around.

'How are the business plans?' I asked.

'Honestly, I've been too busy to do much about it. Work is manic. Maybe after the summer it'll ease up. But I'm too busy for all that stuff right now.'

'That's a shame,' I said.

It was a shame. But it wasn't much of a surprise. Too often, I'd see people sweep aside their biggest goals and priorities in favour of being 'busy'. It's easy to be busy with other, seemingly more urgent things. But key to becoming successful is prioritising the things that matter the most - the tasks and activities that will help you move forwards, in the direction of your goals. If you don't dedicate time to those really important tasks and activities - even when life is busy - you're never going to reach those goals.

MAKING TIME FOR THE THINGS THAT MATTER

I'd said as much to my Rat Racer friend dozens of times, and I said it again.

'Easy for you to say,' he replied. 'You've got this quiet space to work. A team of people who work for you who you can delegate stuff to.'

'But I still have to put the work in. I still have to be really disciplined and do the things that I know will contribute to my success, even when I don't necessarily feel like doing them. It's on me to keep my motivation up. This helps,' I said, pulling up my dream board list on my phone. 'This reminds me of my priorities and the things I want, and makes me more motivated to keep at it and take action. But it's a daily choice, you know. I choose to make time for the stuff that matters.'

'Say I'm really pushed for time . . . which I am,' George said. 'What's the one thing I can do every day to help me?'

I thought for a moment. 'Probably mindfulness, because you can apply it instantly, in any moment, anywhere. I may not make the effort to properly meditate daily, but I use mindfulness every single day. When I tune into the present moment, it stops my mind running amok and helps me feel calmer and more positive. I think that would help a lot when you're feeling like life is too busy. It's so easy to get hung up on what's happening next, or some future thing that may never happen. Just try to tune into the present moment as often as you can.'

'I could do with more of that,' George agreed.

'It's a start, at least. Something to build upon. Then you'll probably be more inclined to carve out time for other techniques, like visualisation and positive affirmations, because you've seen the benefits of mindfulness.'

He nodded, looking around as he did so. 'It's a good yurt,' he said. 'I wouldn't mind something like this one day.'

'Take a picture,' I said. 'Put it on your dream board. Every time you feel like you're too busy to work on your business plan, look at the picture and imagine yourself being your own boss, working somewhere like this.'

George took out his phone and snapped two pictures: one of the inside of the yurt, and the other looking out the window, at the woodland beyond.

BUILDING YOUR OWN SUCCESS-BOOSTING ROUTINE

There's no one cookie-cutter daily routine that you can follow that will bring you success and wealth. The tools I've laid out so far in this book can all be dipped into on a daily basis, or not, depending on what resonates with you.

At least at first, I recommend making time for some or all of these techniques on a daily basis, until they become second nature. That's what I did when I was initially learning these techniques.

I'd get up early and spend around 20 minutes in my office, looking at my dream board, visualising my goals, repeating my positive affirmations and doing a little meditation. And every evening, I'd read something that contributed to my continual education, make sure I kept to my wind-down, sleep-friendly evening routine, and practise gratitude before going to sleep.

Over time, I found that I didn't necessarily need to meditate every single morning, because the benefits lasted for one, two or even three days at a time. But, having learned the technique and made a habit of it, I know I can always dip into meditation whenever I need to.

I still aim for a daily practice of visualisation, affirmations, gratitude and mindfulness. But if I don't get to all of them on a given day, it's fine. I know these tools are there for me when I need them because I took the time to learn them and build those habits in the first place. Now, even if it's been a couple of days since I last visualised my goals, for example, I can quickly settle back into a visualisation exercise because I've done it so many times in the past. By now, it's like riding a bike or driving a car.

My advice to you is to aim for the same. Aim to become adept enough at these mindset techniques so that you can easily draw upon them, whether it's as part of a formal morning or evening practice, or in a more ad hoc way when you need them most.

Ultimately, there are no hard and fast rules on what to do when. You should find your own way that works for you. The only set-in-stone rule here is that you dedicate time to these mental health and mindset strategies. Make that decision to devote time to educating and developing yourself. Commit to it. That's the first step in building a routine that works for you - committing to the process. Even when life is busy. Especially then!

STAYING MOTIVATED

Learning these techniques and starting to use them is kind of the easy part. The tricky part - and the part where most people fall down - is sticking to them. The hard part is continuing to make time for these practices when you have a growing to-do list.

How can you overcome this challenge? The answer lies in keeping your motivation up. Because when you're motivated to do these things, to work on your personal development, you're much more likely to keep at it.

Here are some tricks that have helped me stick at success-boosting habits for the long term:

- Stay focused on your 'why'. Why did you pick up this book in the first place? Why do you want to escape the rat race and become a successful entrepreneur? For me, it was all about freedom - freedom to be my own boss, work when and where it suits me, and have more quality time with my family. Being wealthy for the sake of it isn't much of a motivator, so think hard about your real reasons for wanting a more abundant life. Identify your why and keep reminding yourself of it.

- Create a dream board and pin it up somewhere prominent, somewhere you'll see it every day. Your dream board can just be a list of goals that you want to achieve, or you can pretty it up with aspirational pictures - such as the kind of house you want to live in, or the beautiful places you want to visit.

- Carve out that time. Like I said, I've made a habit of dedicating 15-20 minutes in the morning so I can have a bit of quiet time to practise these rituals. It doesn't have to be morning for you. It could be in the evening, on your lunchbreak, on Sunday mornings, or whenever.

- Build up momentum by focusing on smaller goals as well as the big ones. Try using the law of attraction, visualisation and affirmations to manifest a smaller goal. Believe me, when you manage to achieve that goal, it will spur you on to manifest the next, bigger goal.

- If you can, invest in life coaching. Working with a life coach has really helped me put these tools into practice and stay committed to my journey. More recently, I've also started working with an accountability coach, who makes sure I prioritise my strategic goals and make time for tasks that contribute to those goals. It's not an option for everyone, I get it, but it's something that has helped keep me focused.

- Be kind to yourself. The law of attraction teaches us that thoughts - negative or positive - become things. So when life doesn't go to plan - say, if you let your routine slip a bit, or it's taking longer than you expected to achieve a goal - don't react from a place of negativity. When you're hard on yourself, you're only attracting more negativity your way. Be kind. Remind yourself of all the amazing things you've achieved so far and recommit to the journey ahead.
- Verbalise your intentions. If I tell my loved ones that I want to achieve a certain goal, I know I'll be more likely to achieve it. If I don't, they'll keep on at me (in a good way)! Sometimes, peer pressure is a positive thing. Who can you enlist to help keep you honest?

A FEW TOOLS TO HELP YOU ON YOUR WAY

Internal discipline is great, but you can also use practical tools to keep your motivation up and help ensure you stay committed to your success-building routine.

Here are a few ideas for tools (some technology, some more old-school tools) that will make your success-building routine easier:

- Your dream board. Worth a mention again because it's such an important motivator.
- Your phone calendar and reminders (or old-school diary). I find it helps to diarise time for personal development and set reminders for the things that matter to me. If I know I've got a really hectic work day coming up, for example, I might block out 20 minutes in the middle of that day to do some mindfulness or go for a walk. I'll also set regular reminders that tell me to take a deep breath or list a few things that I'm grateful for. Sounds funny, I know, but it really helps.
- The ThinkUp app. I mentioned this in the positive affirmations chapter, but allow me to mention it again. (I'm not sponsored by them or anything, I just love this app.) With ThinkUp, I can easily keep my favourite positive affirmations with me and play them wherever I am. I'll play them while I'm brushing my teeth, while I'm in the car, just before an important meeting, or any other moment when I need a boost.

- Don't forget, there are also apps like Headspace, Calm and Insight Timer that will help you practise meditation and mindfulness.
- The Motivate app. This handy app offers up daily inspirational quotes. If you enjoy those inspirational quotes that frequently pop up on social media, this is a good app for you.
- The TED app. Love a good TED Talk? Then I recommend you check out this app, which features thousands of TED talks. Perfect for squeezing a shot of inspiration or education into a busy day while you're on the move.

DAILY ROUTINE LESSONS FROM THE RAT RACER AND THE EXTRAORDINARY MILLIONAIRE

- The Rat Racer prioritises being busy over the things that matter.
- The Extraordinary Millionaire prioritises those tasks and activities that move them closer to their goals.
- The Rat Racer goes all out on a new routine for the first few weeks, then quickly loses motivation.
- The Extraordinary Millionaire knows that they have to keep working at it. They make a conscious choice to commit to their personal development. And they keep their motivation up using tools like their dream board.

I've no doubt whatsoever that the mindset tools laid out in this first half of the book helped get me where I am today, writing this book in my yurt, overlooking my beautiful woodland. Techniques like mindfulness, meditation, visualisation and positive affirmations set me up for success and kept me on the path towards building an abundant life. But, of course, all the time I was learning and perfecting these techniques, I was also growing my business and building my wealth. So with that in mind, let's move onto the second half of this book, where we'll explore the financial and business principles that allowed me to escape the rat race, become a successful entrepreneur and build my wealth.

Part II
Extraordinary
Entrepreneurship

LESSONS FOR SUCCESS AND FINANCIAL FREEDOM

'Being rich is having money; being wealthy is having time.'

–MARGARET BONNANO

Chapter 9

Rethinking Your Attitude to Money

'Money really is the root of all evil,' George said, tutting at the TV as the news reporter described the latest political scandal involving some oligarch or other paying for access to MPs.

He switched over to a more kid-friendly channel and we left our youngest daughters to their afternoon play date.

'You don't really believe that?' I asked. 'That money is evil.'

He shrugged. 'I don't know. Seems like a lot of powerful, wealthy people are up to no good. And don't even get me started on the tax-dodging corporations that set up shop here and don't pay their fair share.'

'Most of them are acting within the law, though,' I said. 'If you want to get mad at someone, get mad at the government for creating tax structures that allow corporations and a super-wealthy minority to pay as little tax as possible. You have to remember, though, that those wealthy individuals and corporations bring other benefits - employment, investment, etc. The government wants to attract that money into the country, and favourable tax structures is one way to do it.'

'Well, I still think money causes more problems than it solves. There's a good reason people say it's the root of all evil,' my Rat Racer friend grumbled.

'I disagree,' I said. 'It's usually people who don't have money and want more of it who say money's bad. Someone famous, I think it was George Bernard Shaw, said, "*Lack* of money is the root of all evil." That seems truer to me.'

George laughed at that. 'I didn't take you for a *Wall Street,* greed is good, Gordon Gekko type.'

'I'm not talking about greed, or screwing people over, or illegally dodging tax,' I said. 'I'm just saying that money in and of itself isn't bad.'

TURNING TRADITIONAL BELIEFS ABOUT MONEY ON THEIR HEAD

George's attitude to money is one that I see time and time again. That money is bad. It's at the root of all bad things. But money is just money. It's not inherently good or evil. We need to differentiate between money and the *use* of money.

'Sure, a lot of rich, powerful, unscrupulous people do crappy things,' I said to my Rat Racer friend. 'But a lot of wealthy people give back to their communities. It's like the law of attraction teaches us, if we give more, we get more. That goes for money as well as positive vibes.'

'Well, good, bad or neutral, money isn't the be-all-and-end-all,' George sniffed.

This is another thing I'd often hear people say - that money isn't all that important. They'd protest, usually a little too hard, that they didn't really care that much about money.

'Listen, money matters,' I said, seriously. 'It doesn't matter more than my family or my health, but there's no point pretending it's not important. More often than not, that's something people who *don't* have money will say, that they don't care about money. But people who have money know that it buys them freedom and choice. Freedom to escape the rat race. The choice of how they spend their time. That's hugely important. I'm surprised to hear you saying that. I thought you wanted to quit your job and work for yourself?'

'I did,' George said.

'Then you need to reframe how you think about money. Because, used properly, money buys you the things that really matter in life - more time for the things you love and more freedom, without being constrained by a 9 to 5 job or a paycheque . . .'

I paused for a minute as George's words caught up to me.

'Hang on, did you say you *did* want to work for yourself? Meaning you don't anymore?'

'I don't know,' George sighed. 'I've been headhunted for this job at another company. It'd be a step up. I'd be overseeing the whole European territory. It's a great opportunity. And there's a serious pay bump.'

'Funny how money matters whenever there's a chance of having more of it,' I smiled.

'Alright, alright,' he acknowledged. 'You've got me there.'

'Seriously, though, is this job what you really want?' I asked. 'You'd be giving up on, or at least postponing, a dream you've had for as long as I've known you.'

'Like I said, it'd be a serious pay rise. It's hard to turn down,' my Rat Racer friend replied.

And that's the problem with working for money.

MAKE MONEY, DON'T EARN IT

There are a lot of things that differentiate wealthy people from the not-so-well-off people. The money flowing into their bank accounts. The kinds of cars they drive and the houses they live in. Where they go on holiday.

But the biggest differentiator of all is this: wealthy people make money whereas the not-so-well-off have to earn it. People stuck in the rat race, like my friend George, are working to survive. George wanted to quit the rat race, but he had a mortgage and bills to pay. And that kept him chained to his career, whether he liked it or not. It kept him always seeking that next promotion and pay rise, so he could earn more money and keep the train on the tracks. He feared leaving his job and starting his dream business because he worried about not being able to pay his bills.

I, on the other hand, didn't work to earn money. My property portfolio made money for me. I had rental properties that generated an income. And I had developments underway that would generate capital to buy more income-producing assets in future. I was making money, not earning it - multiplying money with money by investing in assets.

It's the old 'make your money work for you,' adage. Whereas most people are stuck in the reverse, working for their money. As Robert Kiyosaki puts it in his bestselling book, *Rich Dad, Poor Dad*, 'The rich don't work for money. The poor and middle class work for money.'

So, while George had to be out the door at the same time each morning, and came home at the same time each night, often exhausted and uninspired. I had a very different routine. Of course there's some work involved in making money - it's not like I was sitting around in my pants watching daytime TV all day. But I wasn't beholden to a 9 to 5 job to earn money to survive. Importantly, I could focus my time and efforts on the parts of my business that I most enjoyed, and allow others to take care of the parts that I either wasn't qualified to do, or just didn't enjoy as much. That's the beauty of making money versus earning it - freedom and choice.

Importantly, I had the freedom to work on my continual education.

'I was just like you,' I said to George. 'When I was working in the City in my early twenties. I was working to earn money. It wasn't until I started renting out the spare rooms in my house, and got my first taste of passive income, that I saw a different path. That's when I quit my job, vowed never to go back to the corporate life, no matter how bad it got, and started working on my education instead.'

George rolled his eyes. 'Not this again.'

We'd spoken often about the importance of a learning mindset and I'd leant him many a book to help him on his entrepreneurial journey. '

'It's true!' I said. 'That little bit of passive income meant I had the time and freedom to start learning about different property strategies and ways of generating more income from property. I didn't have tons of capital to buy more properties back then. So I had to find ways to make money from property that would give me the capital I needed to actually buy properties. I needed to learn different property strategies and start learning to separate the good property deals from the bad ones, so that I could find the sorts of deals that investors would be interested in. I was working on my education so that I could present credible, attractive opportunities to investors – people much richer than me! So that they'd trust me with their money, which I'd then invest in properties that would generate both a return on their investment plus an income for me. And I'd then use that to build my own capital so I could buy my own properties. By working to learn, I was learning to make money. And make money work for me.'

'But you were younger then,' George said. 'No family to support. You had the luxury of focusing on your education. I've got three kids and a mortgage and an ever-rising cost of living. This isn't the time for me to start a business and take the risk of my income dropping. I need to be earning more money, not less.'

'That's the trap, though,' I argued. 'Instead of looking to earn more money by looking for a better-paid job, you should be looking at how you can *make* more money. Get money working for you. Ideally through investing in valuable assets and building your own passive income, like I do with property. And as you make more money, you reinvest it, rather than hold onto it.'

'So you make all that money and you don't even save it?'

THE MYTH ABOUT SQUIRRELING MONEY AWAY

'My money is no good to me sat in a bank account earning 0.25% interest a year,' I said. 'If you're serious about becoming wealthy, you have to reinvest.'

'But what about saving for a rainy day or your old age?' George asked.

'That's what my assets are for. I put my money into assets that provide an income while also appreciating in value. Cash in the bank only goes down in value.'

George looked confused at this.

It's drilled into us that we need to save, save, save. Put money aside because you never know when you might need it.

To put it bluntly, that's terrible advice. Inflation means that the price of things goes up over time. Petrol, food, utility bills, all of it. This means the value of money actually goes down over time, because £1 buys you less than it did before.

'Think of it this way,' I said to George. 'How much does a tank of petrol cost you at the moment?'

'About £80, give or take.'

'And a few years ago?'

More like £50. Maybe £60.'

'And you're getting the same amount of petrol? It just costs you more?'

'Right.'

'Exactly. Your money doesn't go as far because everything gets more expensive. That's fine if your money comes from assets that are also going up in value. But cash in the bank? That's worth less over time, plain and simple. That's why your money should always be invested in assets that will at least keep pace with, but ideally beat, inflation. If you want to grow your wealth, holding onto your cash is a bad idea. If you have a low-interest savings account at the moment, with the way inflation is, you're basically losing money every month.'

'Of course,' I carried on, warming to my theme, 'because of inflation, the future purchasing power of my assets will also be less than it is today. As in, the value of those assets will buy me less in the future than it does today. So it's not totally black and white. But it's still an extremely sensible, profitable way to approach money. Certainly more sensible than putting money away in a bank account. That's why almost all my money is in property.'

'But don't you worry about all that debt?' George asked.

NOT ALL DEBTS ARE CREATED EQUAL

'It's not like I'm talking about having loads of credit card debt or loans,' I said. 'If I have a mortgage on a rental property, yes, strictly speaking that's a big debt. But I prefer to think of it as money invested rather than debt. Because there's a difference between good debt and bad debt. Good debt is a debt that makes you money - like an investment property. That's money invested because it's making you money in return. It's really an asset, when you think about it. Bad debt is something like buying a sofa suite on credit at 28% interest. All that debt is doing is costing you money. It's not earning you anything. It's not appreciating in value. It's just costing you money, month in, month out. A car on finance is the same thing.'

At this point, George glanced out of the window at his wife's new car. His own car was a company car, but his wife got a new car every couple of years on finance.

'Obviously, I've had cars on finance over the years,' I said, reading his mind. 'We all do it. I'm just saying, the more bad debt you have in your life, the more you're locked into the rat race, because you have to pay off that debt each month. More bad debt equals less financial freedom.'

'I hear that,' grumbled George.

'Whereas the good debt on an investment property is being serviced by the rental income that property generates,' I said. 'I don't have to earn a certain amount to pay that mortgage. It's taken care of. Plus, don't forget the debt is getting eroded over time as the value of the property goes up and I build more equity in the property. And at the end of the mortgage, when the debt is paid off, the asset is worth more than I paid for it. It's a win-win. That's why I focus on good debt and try to limit the amount of bad debt I take on.'

'So you're saying the wife and I need to spend less?' George asked. 'We already tightened our belts after building the extension. I don't think we can cut back any more.'

'It's not about cutting spending, as such,' I replied. 'More, it's about spending your money on things that will make you money. And if you want to take on a bad debt - like a car on finance - you'd ideally be paying for that debt with passive income, like income from a property. That way, you're not having to work to earn to service your debts. The money you make through passive income will pay for them.'

'Sounds brilliant,' George said. 'Trouble is, I don't have any passive income to cover my monthly outgoings, so I have to earn my money.'

Lucky for George, I had some tips on getting started with passive income, and how to invest in assets as opposed to liabilities. But more on that in the next couple of chapters . . .

RETHINKING YOUR OWN ATTITUDE TO MONEY

If you've ever caught yourself saying something like 'Money doesn't matter' or 'Money is the root of all evil', I urge you to rethink your stance. In a lot of ways we're hard-wired to think that money is bad, because many of us grow up seeing our parents trapped in the rat race, having no choice but to earn a living, stuck in that cycle of worrying about not having enough and always feeling that they have to earn more. Maybe your parents encouraged you to do well at school and go to university so you could get a good job and earn plenty of money, without realising they were leading you down the same path. I bet they also told you to save your money in the bank for a rainy day.

It's time to unlearn those old ways of thinking about money.

Money isn't bad. It's only money. (Yes, I know there are a few evil billionaires out there and huge corporations making obscene profits by screwing over people and the planet. But we're not talking about them. We're talking about becoming an Extraordinary Millionaire.)

Money buys you more life choices and the freedom to live life how you want. But you won't achieve that freedom if you work to earn your money - if you're always looking for that next pay rise and wondering how you can earn more. I can say from experience that truly wealthy people don't think how they can earn more money; instead, they find ways for their money to make more money. The best way to do that is by investing in assets, instead of liabilities, and by building passive income streams. But I'll talk about those strategies in more detail in the coming chapters.

For now, I want to urge you to invest in your own financial education. Sadly, we're not taught much, if anything, about money at school. We're not even taught the basics, like how mortgages work or why credit card debt isn't great. We don't even talk about money as a society. Not really. Especially in the UK, where it's often seen as rude or vulgar to talk about money.

That's a shame, because we're creating generations of people who have entirely the wrong ideas about money. Education can change that.

That's why my wife and I are already educating our children about money. They each have a GoHenry card (a prepaid debit card for kids, with an accompanying financial education app). We top up the cards with their pocket money, via the app, and then the kids each manage their own money. And our oldest, who's now a teenager, has recently had a valuable lesson in investing money to make money.

It was one of those school projects where you set up a little business to sell homemade products. In her case, making bracelets to sell to schoolfriends. (It reminded me of my first business selling sherbet!)

We could have simply bought our daughter the materials she needed. But instead we had her invest her own money and buy the materials herself, working out how much was a reasonable amount to spend based on how much she would charge per bracelet. She made a few dozen bracelets, sold them to friends, and then calculated her profit at the end, which she got to keep. Projects like this are so valuable because they teach a few basic business principles, but more importantly, it's an early lesson on investing money to make money. I wish more of this was taught in school.

TRUE WEALTH MEANS ESCAPING THE RAT RACE

People often think that their problems will be solved if they have more money. That they'll be happy if only they get that better job earning more money.

But the truth is, you can be rich - as in, have plenty of money coming in - but still not be wealthy. You can be a Rat Racer earning a fabulous salary, but it's not true wealth if you're stuck doing that job to service all your debt and keep an expensive roof over your head. It's not true wealth if you're constantly worried about not having enough money, if you're still trying to earn more and more. It's not true wealth if you could lose it all tomorrow.

True wealth means having the freedom to work tomorrow if you want to, or not work tomorrow if you'd rather do something different. It means having the financial knowledge to make your money work for you, so that you have genuine financial freedom and security. That's what being an Extraordinary Millionaire means.

Basically, if you think having pots of money will solve all your problems and create a fantastic life, you'll be sorely disappointed. It's how you make that money and what you do with it (i.e. reinvesting it) that counts. And that's why you need to build up your financial education, by immersing yourself in as many resources as possible on wealth-creation strategies, entrepreneurship, investing, passive income, property, and so on (head back to Chapter 7 for more tips on continual education).

A QUICK WORD ON TAX

Tax is a good example of why financial education is so important. Again, I'm not talking about illegal tax-dodging schemes. But there are ways of being more tax-efficient, so that your money can better work for you. Part of learning about this involves working with knowledgeable advisers who can help save you tax (in a legal way, of course).

Typically, people who have a negative view of money are those people who haven't educated themselves about how to make money and make money work for them. These same people will often complain that wealthy people pay less tax than them. As a proportion of income, that's probably true, but wealthy people still pay an awful lot of tax.

The reason wealthy people pay less tax (proportionally) is because they pay for the right advisers. People who help them protect their wealth while staying on the right side of the law. So one tip I have for you is to invest, not just in your own education, but also in quality advisers - in this case, accountants - who will help you with information and practical stuff. Over time, as your wealth grows, don't be shy about upgrading these advisers. I've certainly upgraded my advisers as I've grown wealthier, working with more experienced firms who are used to dealing with more complex business and tax structures. Read more about working with advisers in Chapter 12.

Before we move on, I recommend you take a long hard look at how you think about money. Do you recognise that feeling of always needing to earn more, to get a better job so you can increase your earnings? Do you think about cutting your spending, instead of how to make more money? Do you differentiate between the good and bad debt? If you're stuck in this cycle of working to earn, you're certainly in the majority. But the point of this chapter is to tell you it doesn't need to be that way. Changing how you think about money is a major step on the path to wealth, freedom and living an extraordinarily abundant life.

FINANCIAL LESSONS FROM THE RAT RACER AND THE EXTRAORDINARY MILLIONAIRE

- Someone trapped in the rat race will often speak negatively of money - 'money is the root of all evil' - while simultaneously wanting more of it!
- Someone with an Extraordinary Millionaire mindset knows that money buys freedom and choice. Freedom to leave the rat race behind. Genuine choices on how you spend your time.

- The Rat Racer *earns* money.
- The Extraordinary Millionaire *makes* money. They multiply money with money, by investing in assets that generate income for them.
- The Rat Racer works to earn money and survive. And as such, they're always seeking that next promotion and pay rise - whatever will help them earn more money.
- The Extraordinary Millionaire works on their education, always learning new ways to make their money work for them.
- The Rat Racer squirrels money away in a savings account for a rainy day.
- The Extraordinary Millionaire knows that cash in the bank is only decreasing in value as the cost of everything else goes up. That's why they invest their money in assets that go up in value.
- The Rat Racer doesn't distinguish between good debt and bad debt.
- The Extraordinary Millionaire knows that good debt is debt that makes you money. Bad debt is debt that costs you money. More bad debt means less financial freedom, because it locks you into the rat race.
- The Rat Racer isn't interested in learning about money. They think if they have more money, all their problems will be solved and that'll be that.
- The Extraordinarily Millionaire knows it's how you make money and what you do with it that matters. You can be rich and have a huge salary, but if you're trapped in the rat race, having to earn that fat salary to service all your debts, continually worried you'll lose it all, that's not true wealth. Wealth is freedom. That's why the Extraordinary Millionaire invests in their own financial education.

Building on this notion of good debt and bad debt, one of the biggest financial lessons anyone can learn is to properly differentiate between assets and liabilities. And no, the house that you live in doesn't count as an asset. Read on to find out why . . .

Chapter 10

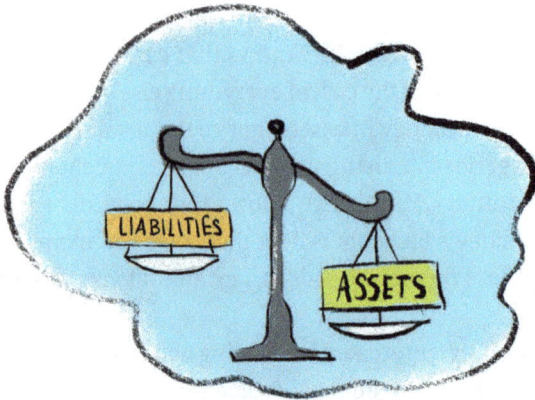

Investing in Assets, Not Liabilities

'It's beautiful,' I said to my Rat Racer friend as he showed me the photos on Rightmove. 'Nice big garden.'

George had taken the new job he was headhunted for, taken the juicy pay rise, and was now looking at buying a bigger house.

'It's a stretch,' he admitted. 'Our mortgage would almost double each month. But I figure that's okay. I'll be earning enough and it's an asset, after all.'

I didn't want to rain on his parade, but he could tell from my face that I disagreed.

'You don't think it's worth the money?' he asked.

'It's not that,' I reassured him. 'It's a lovely property in a great area. Seems a fair price for what it is. And I'm sure it'll go up in value.'

'So, what's the problem?'

'It's just that it's not an asset.'

George screwed up his face. 'Excuse me? Aren't you Mr "Invest in assets. Invest in property"?' He mimicked my voice.

I laughed. 'I am. But *that*,' I pointed at the photos on his phone screen, 'isn't an investment property, is it? It would be your family home.'

'It's still an asset, though. Your home is your biggest asset.'

'Respectfully, no, it's not. It's your biggest liability.'

'I don't get it,' George shook his head. 'You literally just moved to your dream house, with all that space and land. And you're telling me not to do the same thing?'

'I'm not saying don't buy the house,' I said. 'Of course you should buy the home of your dreams, if you can comfortably afford it. Go for it. We don't regret buying our home for a second. It's just that I don't think of my home - the home my family and I live in - as an asset. And neither should you.'

REDEFINING ASSETS AND LIABILITIES

Seeing your home as a huge asset it one of the biggest financial myths out there. But it's so prevalent. George was only repeating what he'd been told a thousand times before, often by experts on the TV. I used to think the same thing about my first home, until I started renting out spare rooms in that property and began actually making money from it. That's when I realised it had, up until that point, only been a liability (financially speaking).

There's nothing wrong with that – buying a home is certainly better than renting – but it's important to know the difference between an asset and a liability.

'A house is only an asset if it generates an income for you,' I explained. 'And since you won't be generating an income from this house – in fact, it'll cost you money every month – it's obviously a liability. That's a much better way of thinking about assets and liabilities: an asset makes money for you, while a liability takes money from you.'

'Think of it this way,' I went on. 'Your net worth isn't the value of your property, not if you have a mortgage on it. Say you own a £500k property, but you only have £100k equity in it, the rest is all mortgage. Your net worth is really £100k, not the £500k that you think you have. When you hear about the net worth of people on the Rich List, that's what their net worth is – it's the value of all their assets minus their liabilities.'

'But the house will go up in value,' George argued. 'So our net worth will go up over time, right? It will make us money in the long run.'

'Yes and no, because unless you sell that home and downsize to a much cheaper property in a much cheaper area, you're not going to reap that profit. As that house goes up in value, so too do other properties that you might move to in future. The whole market will probably have gone up. So, even though you'll have equity from your home, you'll probably still need to take on more debt if you ever want to move. It's not really putting money in your pocket, is it? Not unless you sell it way in the future, once you've paid off all the debt on it, and move to, say, a cheap little property abroad that costs you next to nothing to run, and live off the profit.'

The trouble is, I explained to George, too many people rely on their family home to act as their pension. But like I said, unless he *drastically* downsized and moved to a significantly cheaper area (realistically, another country, the way things are going in the UK), he'd still have to find the money for various outgoings after he retired. Sure, by that time he would (hopefully) own the house outright, but it wouldn't be making him any money each month, and in fact it would still be costing him money, even without the mortgage. So how would he cover those expenses and still live comfortably?

More than that, it's a missed opportunity. Putting all their eggs in the 'my home is my biggest asset' basket stops people like George from seeking out other investment opportunities that would serve them better for the future.

'So, what, there's no point buying a home ever?' George asked.

'Oh no, you should always buy rather than rent, if you can afford it. You just need to understand that what you're taking on is a liability, not an asset.'

'But how does that understanding actually help me, when I still need somewhere to live? I still need to buy a house for my family to live in?'

'To be fair, though,' I said. 'You don't necessarily need to buy a bigger house. You want to, and that's cool. But you don't *need* to move house. All it's doing is locking you into the rat race for longer.'

It's something I've seen time and time again. Someone gets a new job earning more money, so they buy a bigger house, take on a bigger mortgage, get a newer car on finance, go on nicer holidays . . . They spend all the extra money they're earning on more stuff. They pick up more and more liabilities like a magnet picking up metal shavings. Which means they have to continue earning money to service those liabilities. Worse, because they have so many liabilities - basically, they're spending every penny they earn - they never have the spare capital to invest in assets that would get them out of that vicious cycle.

'But you've done exactly the same thing,' George protested. 'You could have stayed in the house next door but you chose to move to a bigger house in the country.'

'Yes, but I'm not locked into the rat race to pay for it,' I said. 'And that's the key difference. If you're going to take on liabilities, like a mortgage or a car on finance, you should be paying for those liabilities with passive income from assets, not earned income from a job. We didn't move to our dream home until I'd accumulated enough income-earning assets to comfortably cover the mortgage and still have plenty left over to reinvest in other assets. If you take on a liability like a big house and pay for it out of your earnings, you're trapped in the cycle of having to work to earn, just so you can cover your commitments every month. There's no way out.'

Bottom line, of course I had liabilities. Almost everyone does. But my liabilities weren't paid for with earned income. And crucially, I was accumulating assets all the time, whereas my Rat Racer friend was only accumulating liabilities.

This is why people stuck in the rat race never become wealthy, and wealthy people more often than not get wealthier. Because the wealthy are constantly investing in assets that make them more money, and they then reinvest that money in more assets - rather than simply taking on more liabilities.

HOW TO ACQUIRE ASSETS WHEN YOU DON'T HAVE THE CAPITAL

'I get what you're saying,' George said. 'But you're in the fortunate position of having investment properties that provide you with an income. I don't have the money to buy even one investment property. So I'm stuck taking on more liabilities, aren't I? And I'm stuck working to pay for them.'

'Not necessarily,' I said. 'I didn't have a lot of capital at first, barring the bit of money I got from renting out the spare rooms in my house. But there are low-capital strategies out there like rent-to-rent - where you rent a property and sublet it to tenants, earning more in rent than you're paying on it.'

'Sounds dodgy,' George said.

'Obviously you have to be upfront with the landlord and get permission. But in my experience, when you present yourself as a property professional - someone who can take this rental property off the landlord's hands, sublet it and manage all the tenant stuff for them - many are happy for you to do so. All most landlords want is their rent paid reliably and zero hassle.'

George looked interested.

I continued, 'So let's say I have five rent-to-rent properties that cost me £5k a month in rent and bills. But I'm renting them out on a room-by-room basis, which is always a better way to earn rental income, so I'm actually earning £9k, maybe even £10k a month in total rental income.'

'But you don't own those properties,' George pointed out. 'So they're not your assets.'

'They're not my personal assets. But they could be considered business assets because they're making money for my property business. And that money will help me acquire more assets in future. See? Or, another way I might grow my capital is by working with investors. That way, they're the ones providing the capital to invest in the assets, but I'm the one doing the work - finding the properties, doing the renovation and managing them. Afterwards, if we sell, we split the profits and, boom, I've grown my capital so I can invest in assets of my own. Some investors are happy for us to keep the assets for longer-term rental income, in which case I have ongoing passive income AND a share of the asset value as well. It's a true win-win relationship!'

'You make it sound so easy,' George said.

'Well, it's not an overnight thing,' I admitted. 'I'm not saying anyone can quit their job and become an overnight millionaire. You have to be prepared to do a lot of learning, and most people embark on this journey while also holding down a paying job, at least at first. So you have to be determined. But my point is lack of capital doesn't have to hold you back from growing your wealth.'

WHY INVEST IN ASSETS INSTEAD OF LIABILITIES?

One word: freedom.

Freedom to choose how you spend your time. True, you probably won't be able to give up work entirely (even passive income generally requires some sort of effort, contrary to what some unethical property gurus might tell you). But when you spend your money on assets, rather than liabilities, you're able to do more of the things you love – whether that's working on your business, spending time with the family, fishing, or whatever. You have more freedom to focus on the things on your dream board.

To put it another way, when you invest in assets, you're more likely to escape the rat race for good. As such, investing in assets is one of the main things that separates the wealthy from the not-wealthy.

That's not to say all liabilities are inherently bad. I'm certainly not saying that you shouldn't buy a house. But I am saying that, when you take on liabilities, you should first and foremost know that what you're taking on *isn't* an asset. And any liabilities that you do take on should ideally be paid for with passive income.

So if you want the nice house with the pool, that's great. But accept it's a liability and aim to accumulate enough assets – assets that generate enough income – to pay for that liability. Otherwise, you have no choice but to continue *earning* money through a job.

At the very least, you don't want to take on so many liabilities that you're trapped in the rat race forever. The more liabilities you take on, the less financial freedom you have. Remember, assets mean financial freedom.

What sort of assets are we talking about? Anything that makes money is an asset. In my case, I focus on property. Build-to-rent properties, houses of multiple occupation (or HMOs for short), commercial conversions, serviced accommodation, new-build property developments, and so on. Of course, there are costs associated with taking on these investments (mortgages, development costs, property management fees, etc.) but they make more money than they cost. And that's the key.

Basically, any sort of passive income business (and that includes invest-ment properties) could be considered an asset. Shares are an asset, too, of course. But I consider them a higher-risk asset in that - in my opinion, at least - you're much more at the mercy of short-term market conditions than you are with property.

WHERE TO START?

Attitude is the first step on your journey to investing in assets. Adjust how you think about assets and liabilities and always be clear on which is which. Just reframing how you think about assets and liabilities can very often help you reduce the number of unnecessary liabilities you take on - especially if you previously (and mistakenly) thought of those liabilities as assets.

Next stop is education, education, education! My advice is to first hoover up every scrap of free or cheap content and advice that you can on investing in assets and building passive income streams. The next chapter is a good start, as are online forums, Facebook groups and other online resources. Then move on to paid-for books and perhaps a training course from a reputable investor with a proven and demonstratable track record in their field. Finally, seek out a great mentor that you resonate with and who has 'been there and got the t-shirt'. Learning from their past experiences and professional relationships will help you fast-track your own journey to success.

You'll also need a healthy dose of patience and the ability to think outside the box - especially when you don't have a lot of capital to invest. As I explained to my Rat Racer friend, it is possible to get started without a lot of capital, but don't expect to be an overnight success. The good news is, all the time you're slowly building capital and acquiring assets, you're also building your knowledge and connections - which will make growth much easier in future.

ASSETS AND LIABILITIES LESSONS FROM THE RAT RACER AND THE EXTRAORDINARY MILLIONAIRE

- The Rat Racer believes their family home is an asset.
- The Extraordinary Millionaire sees their family home as a liability. They define an asset as something that makes them money, while a liability costs money. An investment property is an asset, but the family home? No.
- As the Rat Racer's earnings go up, rather than invest in more assets, they accumulate more and more liabilities. A bigger house, a flashier car, etc. All the time kidding themselves that they're accumulating assets. The truth is they're trapped in the rat race having to pay for all those commitments.
- The Extraordinary Millionaire isn't averse to taking on liabilities. But they take them on fully aware of the difference between an asset and a liability. And crucially, they ensure their liabilities can be paid for by passive income from their assets - so they're not locked into the rat race.
- Short on capital, the Rat Racer doesn't see a way to acquire assets. They believe it's beyond their reach.
- The Extraordinary Millionaire learns creative ways to grow their capital, so they can invest in even more assets in future.

Understanding the difference between assets and liabilities is one thing. But how do you put that into practice and actually invest in assets that will pay for your liabilities? The answer lies in passive income. Which brings us onto the next tool in the Extraordinary Millionaire toolkit . . .

Chapter 11

Focusing On Passive Income

'What do you want to be when you grow up?' I asked my Rat Racer friend's middle daughter.

'A YouTuber,' she answered automatically.

I smiled. All my daughter's friends seemed to have similar ambitions. To be a YouTuber or social media influencer.

'And you?' George nodded at my daughter. 'Will you be following your dad into the property game?'

My daughter screwed up her face. 'No, I'm going to be a YouTuber, too.'

'I don't get it,' George said as we wandered into the house and left the girls to run off into the woodland. 'All her classmates want to be YouTubers.' He shook his head, sadly.

'What's up with that?' I asked.

'It's hardly a proper job,' George said.

'And what do you want her to do instead?' I asked. 'Get a job working 40-odd hours a week making someone else rich? At least YouTube is entrepreneurial.'

'She'll end up broke and living with us forever,' he moaned. 'Very few people make money off social media. She should focus on getting a proper education, and choosing a good, steady career.'

'And locking herself into the rat race forever?' I asked. 'It's funny. We're telling our kids the exact opposite.'

PASSIVE INCOME IS THE PATH TO WEALTH

George looked aghast. 'You're not encouraging this YouTube nonsense?'

'If she wants to do YouTube as a career, then that's fine with me. So long as she approaches it like a proper business venture, finds a successful niche, and so on, I'm all for it. I'd rather she did that than working for someone else.'

'What, even a really good career like being a lawyer or doctor or something? You wouldn't want her to do that?'

'She can be whatever she wants,' I said. 'But I always tell my kids that if they want to have real freedom - financial freedom and, you know, life freedom - then they have to have their own business. It doesn't need to be a high-maintenance business. Property investing is a business that can be very hands-off if you want it to be. Whatever profession my kids choose to go into, I encourage them to work for themselves. If they ultimately decide to go and work for someone else, that's fine, if it makes them happy. But it certainly won't be because they think it's their *only* option. They know from watching me and my wife that you can generate wealth without having to work all hours.'

'You're talking about passive income?' George asked. It was a topic we'd discussed a lot over the years, as he thought on and off about becoming an entrepreneur. 'You teach your kids about passive income?'

'Of course we do. It's important that they see another path, other than the 9 to 5, working-for-money route. Ideally, we want them to find ways to make their money work for them, just as we have. It's like Warren Buffett said, "If you don't find a way to make money while you sleep, you will work until you die." We don't want them working until they die.'

George sat in stunned silence for a moment. 'But don't you worry about them growing up to be lazy layabouts?'

I had to laugh at that. 'I think you might have the wrong idea about passive income. It's rarely entirely passive, in that some investment of time is needed. But the idea is to generate wealth without putting in the sort of hours you would with a regular job. Low-effort, high-reward is the goal. As opposed to the high-effort, low-reward, pay-the-most-taxes con that is working for someone else. Like, I'm still working three or four days most weeks, with those hours arranged whenever I want, because I'm actively trying to grow my business and create more passive income streams. If I stopped striving for growth, I could easily retire now, in my forties, and just live off the income from my property investments. But where's the fun or challenge in that?'

The look on George's face said he thought it might be quite fun to retire now.

'Besides,' I said. 'I think society has the wrong idea about working. I want to be successful - and I want my kids to be successful - but I just don't believe being successful means you have to work long, unsociable hours or be defined by what you do for a living. Life in the City was like that, an unspoken competition to see who could work the latest every evening to show you were the best employee. On the surface, I was in this highly successful, desirable job that other people would kill for. But I was miserable. And I had no work–life balance. I was only in my early twenties and facing decades more of that lifestyle. It was a horrible thought, to be honest. I'd hate for my kids to be in that situation.'

'So what turned you onto passive income?' George asked.

'In the end, I just decided I deserved better than that. I was renting out a spare room in my house to help cover the mortgage. Then I decided to rent out a second bedroom - and the income from those two tenants was enough to cover my mortgage outright. I was effectively living mortgage-free, which was pretty damn satisfying. So I invested some money and converted my garage to make another rental bedroom, and that took me from covering my mortgage outright to actually making a profit each month. That was my first official bit of passive income. It wasn't much: around £500 profit a month. But it was money coming in through minimal effort on my part. I was hooked. I realised if I just did more of the same, I could be making good money without having to work all hours. So I quit my job altogether and started focusing on property.'

IT'S NOT JUST ABOUT THE MONEY (ALTHOUGH THE MONEY HELPS)

'You quit your job in an investment bank to live on £500 a month?' the Rat Racer said. 'Blimey, I didn't know it was that much of a leap.'

'Yeah, don't get me wrong, I was *scraping* by at first,' I admitted. 'But I knew it was the right thing to do, and that it wasn't all about money.

Passive income is about rethinking the nature of work altogether. For me, at the moment, that means working three or four days a week, with hours that let me drop the kids off at school and be done in time to pick them up. For someone else, it might mean working two days a week, or a few hours every morning, or whatever.'

'Sounds like you're still working pretty hard.'

'Well, it depends on the week. Sometimes I am putting in longer hours, if there's a big deal going through, or we're at a crucial point on a development. Or, like right now, where my company is developing property investing and other wealth-creation courses. That's a lot of work on my part. But I'm doing it all out of *choice*, because I'm excited by those projects. I also have loads of property investments that need hardly any time commitment from me to generate an income. I have an awesome team that handles the day-to-day stuff, like finding and vetting tenants and maintaining the properties. Basically, because of the way I've set up my various business ventures, when I am working, I can focus my time and efforts on those areas where I'm most effective or the things that I enjoy the most. I have the freedom to do that.'

WHY KEEP WORKING AT ALL?

George scratched his head. 'But if you have a team of people who can manage your existing investments for you, and you could effectively retire tomorrow . . . well, why don't you? Why on earth are you still working?'

'That's easy,' I said, without hesitation. 'Because I want to keep growing. Yes, I could automate or outsource everything and just leave the business to tick along, but I enjoy growing. I love the thrill of finding new deals, working with investors to do bigger and bigger developments, and creating win-win deals. I enjoy growing my wealth. And I guess I want to leave a bigger legacy for my kids. I like being able to give back, too. To charity, but also giving more of my time to newbie property investors through things like mentoring, training, putting out YouTube content, writing books, etc. Growing my passive income allows me to do more of that stuff, which makes me happy.'

'God, I'd just retire if I were you,' George said.

'Honestly, I can't see me ever fully retiring,' I admitted. 'I reckon I'll still be putting property deals together or mentoring others when I'm old and grey. Because I love it. Working on building designs. Putting project teams together. Paying it forward to aspiring investors. All that's fun for me. But if someone else just wants to get enough passive income that they can live comfortably for the rest of their life and never have to worry about money again, that's also great. Passive income can totally do that.'

'Hmmm,' George looked thoughtful. 'I definitely think I'd lean more towards the early retirement . . .'

'You might surprise yourself. Because if you find a passive income business that you're really passionate about, it doesn't really feel like work. It *is* work, of course. But it's work that connects to your passion. That's a common myth about passive income - that it's all about retiring early, never working again and playing golf forever. It can be. But it's mostly about having the time and freedom to focus on the things you enjoy most - family and hobbies, obviously, but you might also enjoy growing your business, or working on certain parts of the business and leaving others to do the rest.'

George was, at this point, well established in his new job. He was travelling a lot in Europe and, for the most part, embracing the challenge. But it was taking a toll. He wasn't around as much. More often than not, when my wife and I saw his family, George was travelling or catching up on sleep, or preparing for some big work thing. This was a rare day when all of us could get together. He looked tired.

'That's all well and good,' George sighed, 'but the house move has wiped out the last of our savings and we're mortgaged up to the hilt, so there's not much hope of creating any passive income when I haven't got anything to invest, is there?'

'Oh, I don't know,' I said. 'There are ways of getting started without a lot of capital.'

George raised a tired eyebrow.

'You should think about,' I said to him. 'If you started building some passive income streams now, maybe you could retire early. Or have the time to finally launch your cycling app.'

FAST-FORWARD A FEW DAYS · · ·

George's picture lit up my phone.

I answered the call. 'Hey George, what's up?'

'I've been thinking about what you said. I've done my sums and I reckon if I save really hard for the next six months, cancel my gym membership that I'm not even using anymore, stuff like that, I could probably scrape together £10k.'

'Go on . . .' I said.

'So if I want to turn that into the beginnings of a passive income fortune, what would you recommend?'

'With property?' I asked.

'Yeah, property. I was thinking I could put a deposit down on a buy-to-let mortgage. There are those new blocks going up in the centre aimed at young professionals. One of those flats could earn as much as £1,000 a month in rent.'

'And when the mortgage is paid, how much would you have left over each month?' I asked.

'Probably not much,' George said. 'But it's a start, right?'

'Honestly, George, it's not what I would do,' I said. 'I know that's what a lot of people think of when they think of investing in property - just buying a second property and renting it out, earning just enough to cover the mortgage and keeping the property as a nest egg - but there are better ways to turn £10k into greater wealth for the future.'

'So what would you do with it?' George asked.

'If I was just starting, I'd take that £10k and invest in my education so that I could learn the different property strategies out there. Learn how to work with investors and how to find great properties that investors want to invest in.'

George sounded disappointed. I suspected he was hoping for a quicker fix.

'Look,' I said, 'if you're really serious about growing a passive income stream that lets you give up the 9 to 5 for good, one rental property isn't going to cut it. If I were you, I'd spend, say, two-thirds or even three-quarters of that money on your education - really good-quality courses or mentorship programmes, and then whatever's left over could be the start of a property business.'

'Come on, I can't buy anything or get a mortgage with just a couple of grand left over,' George said.

'No,' I agreed. 'But you could take out a lease on a rent-to-rent property. I've mentioned that before, where you then sublet it to tenants, with the landlord's permission. Or you could start a deal-sourcing business, where you sell property information, basically facilitating property deals by bringing buyers and sellers together. You earn a commission on each deal.'

'I don't want to be an estate agent,' George said.

'There's a difference,' I corrected him. 'A deal-sourcer and an estate agent both sell property information, but while an estate agent might deal with all sorts of properties - residential, commercial, sales, rentals, etc. depending on their specialism - a deal-sourcer focuses purely on investment properties. You find deals that will appeal to investors. Which means it's a great way to connect with investors and build your network. I have a deal-sourcing business as part of my passive income. I wouldn't recommend it if it didn't work for me.'

'I don't know . . .' George said.

'If you're serious about building passive income through property and you don't have a lot of upfront capital, rent-to-rent and deal-sourcing are a couple of brilliant strategies to get you started because you're earning money and learning the industry as you go. You're building your skillset. And, with deal-sourcing, you're building a network of contacts as well as investors who could potentially finance your own property projects in future. I found out early on that working with investors is a great way to grow quickly. They invest in the assets. You find the properties, oversee the renovation, etc. And you get a share of the assets and profits in return. Bit by bit, you grow your capital to invest in your own assets.'

'But I don't know anything about finding good deals for investors,' George said.

'Exactly, that's why you start by investing in your education.'

I could tell George wasn't that enthusiastic. He wanted an overnight way out of the rat race, when no such thing exists. For most people, especially those who don't have a lot of capital behind them, their passive income journey starts while they're still working their regular job. Only after a little while can they actually afford to give up being an employee and start living the passive income lifestyle - whatever that looks like for them.

I was kind of the exception to the rule, in that I quit my job pretty much straight away, when I only had that measly £500 a month to live on. I had to live extremely frugally in the early days, until I built up more passive income, but I managed because I was a young guy with no family to support and no liabilities. I'm assuming most people reading this book aren't in that position, and will most likely start a passive income business as a side hustle. At first, anyway. With a bit of work and the right strategy (or strategies), even a small passive income stream can turn into a generous flow of money. Take it from me: someone who turned £500 a month into a multi-million-pound property portfolio.

With that in mind, let's see how you can create your own passive income.

HOW PASSIVE IS PASSIVE?

Don't be fooled by the name. Unless you fully retire and never put in another hour on your business, passive income is never truly passive. It will always need a bit of management and maintaining to keep the income rolling in. You have to do some work. But, importantly, your money works for you, rather than you working for money. The reward-to-effort ratio is far greater than that in a 9 to 5 job.

Think about it, if you work eight hours in your job, you get paid for eight hours. It's a one-to-one ratio. Passive income, on the other hand, can give you a one-to-many ratio, in that for every hour I spend on my business, I'm generating far more wealth than one-hour's pay. That's why I believe passive income is the only real way to achieve financial freedom, success and an abundant life.

It's also the practical way of implementing everything we learned in Chapter 10, about investing in assets not liabilities. By investing in assets that deliver an income, your money is working for you. (And remember, a business is an asset. We're not just talking about investment properties or other obvious assets. Starting any kind of business that requires minimal effort for the financial reward is a way of both investing in assets and building passive income.)

But anyway, how passive is passive?

There's no one-size-fits-all template here. As I said to my Rat Racer friend, I currently choose to work a good three or four days a week on my business because a) I love it and b) I'm still in the growth phase of my life. In the future, as I get older, I'll no doubt scale that back gradually, but I'll probably always be putting in a bit of effort to keep the passive income flowing and to keep my mind active. It's just that the tasks I choose to focus on, and the amount of time I devote to them, will probably evolve over time.

Your ideal passive income setup may just be a few hours a week. In which case, I highly recommend you read *The 4-Hour Workweek* by Tim Ferriss. It's packed with practical tips on building passive income, and it also talks a lot about the mindset of outsourcing tasks and building systems that do the work for you, so you need only put in a few hours a week to keep things ticking over. *The $100 Startup* is another popular passive income book.

Rather than thinking about the number of hours you want to work, you might instead think of the percentage of income that comes from passive income. Ideally, you should be aiming for passive income to make up as much of your total income as possible. I'd say my passive income makes up about 60% of my income currently, largely coming from rental income, plus some affiliate marketing income (we'll talk more about the different types of passive income later). The rest of my income comes from new developments that my property business has finished and sold, and things like my mentorship programme, courses and book sales (although, don't let anyone tell you you'll get rich from publishing a book!). I find that percentage is a nice balance for me at this time in my life, but in the future, I might want to have, say, 95% of my income from passive income sources that require little effort. You might be gunning for that 95% sooner than me, which is fine. My point is, I'd think more about the percentage of income that comes from low-effort sources, rather than the number of hours you physically have to put in.

So that's the first myth about passive income: that it means you never have to work another day in your life. What are some other key myths?

One is that passive income is an overnight thing. It's not. It's certainly a better way of growing wealth than climbing your way up the corporate ladder. But you probably won't be able to quit your job tomorrow, yelling 'see ya, suckers, I'm off to live the dream' as you sail out the door. (That would be great, though, wouldn't it?)

It takes some time to build up a good level of passive income, which means it may be a while before you're ready to give up the security of your existing income. You don't have to quit at all, if you absolutely love your job. Keep doing your job for the satisfaction it gives you, and let your passive income investments take care of growing your wealth. But I'm assuming most people picking up this book do ultimately want to quit their job and escape the rat race. In which case, I would suggest finding ventures or investments that allow you to keep doing the day job until the passive income is sufficient to quit.

Note that I said 'sufficient to quit' not 'equal to your current salary'. Because, when you do quit, chances are you'll be taking a pay cut at first. That'll hurt. I know, I've been there. But with your time 100% dedicated to your new passive income model, you should be able to increase growth fast, build that income back up, and ultimately far exceed it.

Another common myth is that you need a lot of money to get started. As I explained to the Rat Racer, that's just not true - there are absolutely low-capital ways to get started. Passive income isn't just for those who are already wealthy (although, it's certainly true that most wealthy individuals will have multiple sources of passive income, so there's a definite connection between the wealthy and passive income). As Tim Ferriss argues in *The 4-Hour Workweek,* true wealth comes not just from money, but time and mobility, too. What he means is, wealth isn't just about having money in the bank - it's about freedom.

You don't even need to be particularly business-savvy to get started. I certainly wasn't when I began renting out rooms in my house. My skills and expertise grew over time, often learning the hard way and making mistakes, and so will yours.

PASSIVE INCOME OPTIONS

Think of passive income as another name for 'yield', or the money you make on an investment, but with minimal input required from you for the income to continue to flow in. You invest a little money, and you get money back in return on a regular basis, with minimal involvement from yourself.

Basically, anything that generates money that isn't directly tied to your effort or output is passive income (so, it's that one-to-many ratio, rather than the one-to-one ratio of paid employment). Think of it that way and the options for passive income are pretty broad.

Investing in shares is one example of a passive income stream (albeit normally a fairly low-yield one, requiring more upfront capital to get a return you can fully live off). Personally, I only invest a small amount of my overall wealth in shares, crypto or other securities like currency. I wouldn't want to go any deeper into that sort of investing without fully understanding the markets and micro- and macro-economic factors to an extremely detailed level. That takes an awful lot of time, which I'm not prepared to invest. And I say that as someone who used to work on a trading floor, sitting alongside all the traders. And honestly, the markets just don't interest me to quite the same level as property, and they never really did. It's not my passion and that's why I was so keen to get out all those years ago. I also think it's pretty telling that, when I worked in the City, I rarely saw the traders heavily invest their own money in stocks and shares. More often than not, they put most of their money into other assets, like property.

I'm not ruling shares out for you. If you love getting technical and geeking out, then it could be perfect for you. Just be aware that, to generate serious regular income, you'll need quite a bit of capital to get going with, or be prepared to take a much higher risk with complicated share strategies like derivatives. Basically, it's not for the faint-hearted and much harder to create passive income quickly.

Affiliate marketing websites are another option. This involves generating income (commission, basically) from online adverts and links, with retailers or service providers paying a commission to your site in return for generating traffic and sales for their site. For example, your site might offer discounts and promotional codes for retailers, then you earn a commission when people click through from your site and buy.

I have previously owned one such commission-based business. To set it up, all my team needed to do was create the website itself, build networks with affiliate marketing companies, set up Google AdWords and social media to pull traffic to our site, and we were off. I had a small team in place who ran the admin and sales side of things for me and ensured the site stayed current, so it required little input from me to keep it going. Affiliate marketing is probably the perfect example of a four-hour-a-week business.

If affiliate marketing doesn't grab you, the internet offers tons of other opportunities for passive income businesses. Technology platform businesses and apps can be particularly lucrative, although, unless you're a skilled web developer, there is obviously some upfront investment required to create a quality offering. On the plus side, the possibilities for business opportunities online in this day and age are endless. And with such a level playing field, anyone can enter the market with a great idea and get going.

My passive income model of choice is property. In fact, I believe property is the most accessible and achievable path to passive income for the average person.

BUILDING WEALTH THROUGH PROPERTY

Property is my primary individual area of expertise so, naturally, it's my top recommendation for passive income. And I'm not alone. There's a reason property is many people's first choice for passive income: property is something we can all get our heads around. Whether you're a tenant, a homeowner, living with parents or whatever, we can all understand what makes a property attractive and pleasant to live in. That's what makes property such an accessible passive income choice.

It can create serious wealth, too, if done right. But I think what excites me most about property is the sheer range of sub-strategies for generating wealth. Most people would automatically think of buying and selling the odd fixer-upper for a few grand's profit here and there, or taking on a buy-to-let property. But as I said to my Rat Racer friend, there are many other (and I think, better) ways to build passive income through property.

Some of my favourite strategies include:

- Houses in multiple occupation (HMOs). With this strategy, instead of renting out a property as a single let (as in, to one tenant, couple or family), you rent out each bedroom on a separate tenancy agreement, with communal shared facilities like the kitchen and, sometimes, bathrooms. This delivers significantly more rental yield than a standard, single buy-to-let – sometimes as much as double. I still have a lot of HMOs in my property portfolio, many of which are rented out to young professionals. But the HMO model can also be applied to students and social housing tenants (usually provided by the local council or a local housing association). What I love about HMOs is the low level of risk. Let's say two bedrooms in a five-bedroom HMO sit empty for a couple of months – the good news is, you're still earning income on the other three bedrooms, which will almost certainly cover the mortgage and bills. Whereas if a standard let lies vacant, you're the one left footing the mortgage and bills during any void periods.

- Property development. Not strictly passive income, in that developing a property requires a fair amount of work on your part (even when you have professionals doing all the building work, project management, etc., there's still a lot of effort required to find and develop the best sites) – and, if you sell the property at the end, you get profit but no ongoing income. That's why I mostly follow a build-to-rent model, where I retain the finished property and rent it out. The key thing with property development is to *add value*, and some of the best ways to do that are converting a single unit into multiple units, building on an empty plot of land, or converting a commercial building (such as an office block, shop or care home) for residential use. The latter has been especially fruitful for me.

- Serviced accommodation. This can span anything from letting out rooms or apartments on Airbnb to owning a huge aparthotel. Because you often charge on a per-night model, the income is higher than if you rented out the same unit on a monthly basis. Although this strategy often produces significantly higher revenue, it is also very time consuming and is practically a whole business in itself. So if you're aiming for that all-important passive income, you'll have to set up your serviced accommodation business very carefully.

- Rent-to-rent. This is a really fast-growing area right now and involves renting a property and, with permission, subletting it (ideally as an HMO). It's a great strategy if you don't have the capital to buy property assets – with this strategy, the business itself is your asset.

- Lease options. This is the same as rent-to-rent, except it's written into your contract that you have the option to purchase the property after a certain amount of time. I like this because I earn an income from the property in the short and medium term, but long term - once I've built up a little capital from the rental income - I have the option to acquire it as an asset.
- Generating and selling property leads. Becoming a deal-sourcer or buyer's agent (i.e. sourcing properties for other investors to invest in) is a great way into property, giving you hands-on experience, plenty of learning opportunities and fantastic connections. And it requires little capital.

I still use all of these strategies to this day and highly recommend them. If you want to read more about property investment strategies, check out the educational resources on the Property Forum site - head to www.propertyforum.com/educationalebooks. I'm also the author of *Investing in International Real Estate For Dummies,* which covers all sorts of strategies for building wealth through property. Find it where you find all good books!

I hope these strategies show that you don't necessarily need a huge wad of cash behind you to get started in property. Rent-to-rent, for instance, requires nothing more than the first month's rent and deposit. And if you're savvy, you could scrape that together by lining up tenants before you officially take possession, by negotiating access to the property for viewings with prospective tenants. This means property can be an almost zero-capital way into passive income. With a well-chosen rent-to-rent property in the right location, you could be making up to £2,000 a month in passive income from just one property.

Remember, though, it's only an asset if it brings you profit and passive income. If an investment property doesn't make you money, it's a liability. This is where many landlords fall down. If they neglect their properties or manage them badly, to the point where tenants don't want to rent from them anymore, then, with a mortgage to pay, properties can very quickly become liabilities.

DEVELOPING MULTIPLE STREAMS OF PASSIVE INCOME

I read somewhere that the average millionaire has seven sources of income. And therein lies the real secret of success in passive income: it should come from multiple sources. I feel like I quote Warren Buffett a lot (that's okay, the man knows what he's talking about), but he famously said, 'Never depend on a single income.' I couldn't agree more. That's why I have multiple property businesses and deploy several different property strategies, as listed before.

Some of my business income streams include The Property Forum (which earns income from advertising and provides an educational resource for property investors), and Redbrick Wealth (which generates commission as a sourcing and selling agent, and also sells our own finished development sites). And when it comes to property income, I have a portfolio that spans HMOs, aparthotels, serviced accommodation lets, freehold apartment blocks, and rent-to-rent (although I usually use this as a lead-in to actually purchasing the property on a lease option). I also co-own a beauty salon chain with my wife, which (thankfully for everyone involved) requires little to no input from me other than some marketing guidance from time to time. And by the way, my wife does an amazing job running that business for less than a day a week, generating more passive income for the family.

The advantage of having multiple streams like this is increased financial security. If all your passive income comes from one source, and something threatens that income, you're in trouble. But with multiple streams, you can spread the risk. For example, when the 2008 financial crisis hit, and credit dried up overnight, the parts of my portfolio reliant on property sales were hit hard because people just couldn't get mortgages. However, the rental segment did brilliantly as there were more renters in the marketplace. The cyclical nature of the economy, particularly the property market, means it's always a good idea to have your fingers in as many pies as possible, without spreading yourself too thin, of course.

A QUICK WORD ON OUTSOURCING

Part of creating passive income is investing in the technology and/or people to take care of various activities for you. Trying to do everything yourself is not very passive at all. Besides, according to the famous Pareto principle, or 80/20 rule, 80% of results (sales, income) come from 20% of effort. So why not focus on that results-delivering 20% and eliminate, automate or outsource the other 80%?

That's what I try to do in my business. Why spend my time finding and vetting tenants or dealing with rental agreements, when I have other people who can do a much better job of that for me? My time is much better spent finding sites that are ripe for property development or a specific rental strategy, working with investors to take on bigger projects, and working on activities that help others and boost my personal brand (YouTube and writing this book, for example).

There's a cost associated with taking this hands-off approach, which means you'll inevitably sacrifice some of your income. However, I prefer to think of this as a positive, because the reward for outsourcing work is that I have more time to focus on profit-enhancing activities. Ultimately, it creates greater value for me - and increased income in the long run.

Remember, your time is valuable, so calculate your hourly rate to work out whether outsourcing is worth it. If it costs less to outsource it than to do it yourself, go ahead and outsource it. If it costs more, keep hold of the task until your hourly rate increases or you can find a more cost-effective option.

I talk more about outsourcing and building a fantastic support team in the next chapter.

IS PASSIVE INCOME REALLY WORTH IT?

I can only really talk about my experience, but yes, it's been 100% worth it for me. Assuming you build up to a level of passive income where you no longer need to work 9 to 5, you'll have much greater flexibility, freedom and choice in how you live your life. Even down to *where* you live. These days you can generate passive income from pretty much anywhere in the world. This means my family and I can take off for most of the school holidays if we want to, and I can still keep things ticking over.

Passive income also gives you a chance to connect with your passion. I know I wasn't passionate about my old job. Now, life couldn't be more different. Focusing on passive income allows me to build businesses that excite me, and means I get to concentrate my efforts on the parts of the business that most interest me, or where I have the most impact. I also have plenty of time to indulge my other passions, like travelling with my family, camping, fishing, classic car shows, and the like. Ultimately, I feel as though passive income has allowed me to live life to the fullest. And that's pretty special.

It's not all rosy, of course. You do have to take a slightly longer-term view. Passive income isn't a get-rich-quick scheme. It's a way of thinking and building the right income streams from the start.

Then there's the fact that, once your passive income streams are in motion, you can't just take your foot off the gas. This is a common error in passive income, where people ignore their businesses or investments and then have to step back in when things go wrong, and devote lots of time and energy to getting things back on track. I've done it myself with one of my former lettings management companies that wasn't cutting the mustard. I let things slide for a while, hoping I wouldn't have to step in. But of course I did, and I had to devote much more time than if I'd stepped in earlier. Lesson learned! It's far better to devote time little and often to keeping your passive income projects on track.

TIPS FOR GETTING STARTED

My first and probably biggest tip is to invest in your education. Spend time and effort (and, yes, money) deepening your understanding of the theory behind passive income and learning your chosen passive income field, whether that's property, online businesses, or whatever. Get inspired by other people's successes. Read as many books as you can get your hands on and use their lessons to engineer your own path to success. Head back to Chapter 7 for more on education.

You'll also enjoy your passive income journey much more if you can connect it to your passion. When deciding on your first passive income business, think about how you'd most like to spend your (work) time and what's most interesting to you. I love property. It offers huge diversity of passive income options, it's constantly evolving, and it's just fascinating. So if you aren't sure where your passion lies, I urge you to consider investing in property. If an online or product-based business appeals more, Tim Ferriss's *4-Hour Workweek* is definitely for you.

Another tip is to not fall into the trap of being 'busy'. I hate that word. People fling it around like it's a badge of honour, when really it's just a sign that they're not working smart enough. Be ruthless here. Once you've decided on your first passive income business, write down every task that's involved in getting the business off the ground and keeping it ticking over. Then, work through each task and see if it can be done by a freelancer or technology.

And finally, always be looking for ways to expand and diversify. Passive income is at its most powerful when you have multiple streams coming in on a regular basis. So, once your first passive income venture is up and running, look for new ways to diversify your income portfolio.

Your passive income business probably won't be passive immediately. But don't let that put you off. Rather than a quick fix, think of passive income as a total mindset shift. It's a sustainable way to set up a new business (or adapt an existing business so it requires less involvement from you), invest, build your wealth and create greater freedom for you and your loved ones. I don't know why anyone would do anything else.

PASSIVE INCOME LESSONS FROM THE RAT RACER AND THE EXTRAORDINARY MILLIONAIRE

- Someone with a Rat Racer mindset struggles to see beyond the traditional route of working to make someone else rich.
- The Extraordinary Millionaire knows that to achieve true financial freedom, you have to have your own business - ideally, a low-effort, high-reward business. This is the idea behind passive income. It's a way to invest in assets (not liabilities) that deliver a regular income.
- The Rat Racer thinks passive income means quitting your job and sitting back and doing nothing.
- The Extraordinary Millionaire knows it's a little more involved than that. Most people can't afford to instantly quit their job. And even once they have built up enough passive income to quit their job, keeping that passive income rolling in (and ideally, growing that income) requires some time and effort. It's just that the time and effort spent delivers much greater reward than working for money. The time and effort put in by the Extraordinary Millionaire ensures their money keeps working for them.
- The Rat Racer thinks passive income isn't an option for them because they don't have spare capital to invest in assets.
- The Extraordinary Millionaire knows that an asset doesn't have to be a property or shares - it could be a business. It could be a property business. And there are property strategies like rent-to-rent and deal-sourcing that allow you to earn a passive income - and learn the property industry from the inside - with minimal upfront investment. Besides, the best investment you can make is in your own education and experience.
- A Rat Racer can easily fall into the trap of being too busy in their passive income business. They try to save money by doing everything themselves.
- The Extraordinary Millionaire knows that investing in technology and/or people to take care of various tasks is vital. It frees you up to focus on those activities that you love and will deliver maximum value and future growth.

- If they do manage to achieve a passive income stream, the Rat Racer will sit back comfortably, happy with their one income source.
- The Extraordinary Millionaire knows how important it is to develop multiple streams of passive income over time. Never, ever rely on one single source of income.

I've talked a lot so far in the book about drawing inspiration from others and outsourcing tasks to people who are better qualified. In other words, no entrepreneur is an island. Let's delve a little more into this notion of relationships - specifically, boosting your own success by surrounding yourself with people who are smarter than you . . .

Chapter 12

Surrounding Yourself with People Who Are Smarter Than You

George the ex-neighbour was having one of those proud parent moments.

'Brightest kid in her class, her teacher said. I hope it stays that way when she moves up to seniors next year.'

'Why's that?' I asked.

George looked confused.

I tried again. 'Why does it matter if she's the smartest child in the room?'

'Doesn't everyone want their kid to be the smartest in the class?'

I shrugged. 'Dunno. I wasn't. Matter of fact, when I was her age, I liked having friends who were smarter than me. It meant I didn't slack off. Sometimes, I had to work hard to keep up and I think that was good for me.'

'I just don't want her confidence to take a knock, that's all. She knows she's at the top of her class and that seems to give her a boost. It did for me as well when I was at school.'

I wasn't sure I agreed with him. Because always thinking you're the smartest person in the room isn't necessarily a good thing. I chose my next words carefully.

'Well, if her best friends are anything like I was at school, I'm sure it's giving them a boost, having such a bright friend,' I said. 'That's proven isn't it? That the intelligence of your childhood best friend influences your IQ years later?'

OUR INTELLIGENCE IS INFLUENCED BY OTHERS

'Really?' George replied.

'Yeah, I saw it in some psychology article. Researchers found that the IQ of older teenagers was strongly linked to the IQ of their best friend when they were 11. So, having a brainier friend was associated with higher future intelligence. It's fascinating.'

'That is interesting,' George agreed. 'Do they know why?'

'I don't think it's totally clear-cut, but they adjusted for other factors like the child's own intelligence at age 11, their parents' intelligence, their home environment, and still found a strong link between their childhood best friend's intelligence and their IQ as a teenager. The researchers figured that having a friend who studied and worked hard at school just rubs off, so you're more motivated to study and work hard yourself - and that has lasting positive effects on intelligence. Maybe even all the way into adulthood.'

'Amazing.'

'That's why I think it's okay to not always be at the top of the class. There's a lot we can learn from others, and the sooner we understand that in life, the better. So, basically, if she goes to secondary school and is surrounded by more intelligent children, I wouldn't sweat it. It'll probably be good for her.'

George nodded thoughtfully, then laughed. 'God, my best friend at age 11 was my older cousin Wesley. He was 13. He thought raisins were dead flies. But he was the coolest kid I knew. I used to do his maths homework for him. I probably would've jumped off a cliff if he'd told me to!'

'And where is he now?' I asked.

'He made Captain in the Royal Marines and retired at 40. Started a small brewery down in the West Country. He's doing very well for himself.'

'Who knows, that could've been your good influence from all those years ago,' I laughed.

'Hmm, but what did I get out of it?' George asked with a smile. 'Apart from the odd free crate of IPA now and then?'

He had a point. In their shoes, growing up, I'd rather have been Wesley than George. My guess was Wesley had the good sense to know his strengths and weaknesses, and that hanging out with his clever little cousin was beneficial in more ways than one. Or, I don't know, perhaps the kid just really hated maths and couldn't be bothered to do his own homework.

'Maybe this is where the old "not what you know but who you know" saying originally came from,' I said. 'From knowing you don't know enough - and surrounding yourself with people who know better and can do better?'

George mulled this over for a second. 'I never thought of it that way.'

And why should he? Because the traditional corporate hierarchy doesn't set us up to think this way at all. In the corporate world, unless you get to build your entire team from the ground up, you have no control over the people around you. You never have to think about this stuff. None of it matters. You work with the people you work with, and that's it.

The corporate world also encourages a different attitude to success. For people with the Rat Racer mindset, success is an obvious linear path. You get a good job, then you focus on getting the next promotion, and the one after that. At every stage of his career, George had had his eye on his boss's job. And he still did, even though he was now a boss himself and had people nipping at his own heels. His focus was too narrow.

What's more, George liked being the smartest person in the meeting room and always had. It was hard for him to open his mind to my way of thinking - that recognising you're not the smartest person in the room, and actively seeking out people who are smarter than you, is a strength not a weakness. For people like George, hiring a super-smart team member who could out-perform him in certain areas would be threatening.

I remember one time, years ago, I'd mentioned to George that I'd set up a meeting with a property investor that I admired hugely. This investor was, at that time, operating at a bigger scale than me. I found their path to success inspiring. And I wanted to explore opportunities to collaborate. George was bemused by my approach.

'But they're your rival,' he said. 'You want what they've got.'

I thought his way of thinking was narrow and short-sighted. And he thought I was showing weakness.

'If what you're saying is true,' George said. 'People would only ever hang out with people who were much more successful than them. So why would this super-successful developer want to give you the time of day when you're not more successful than him?'

'It's not necessarily about "success" though,' I said, with added air quotes. 'Because everyone defines success differently. I'm talking about surrounding yourself with people who are smarter than you. They may or may not be richer or more successful than you, but they know something you don't. So, yes, my property business isn't as big as this guy's. I may not be making as much money as him, yet. But I've been building a reputation in areas where he doesn't operate - houses in multiple occupation, commercial-to-residential developments . . . When it comes to these strategies, I'm more expert than him, even though his portfolio is bigger than mine. We can learn from each other. Just as I learn from people in my team all the time. People who really know their stuff on certain topics.'

In other words, when I talked about surrounding myself with people who were smarter than me, I was referring to two main types of people - those who inspired me and spurred me on to do better, and those people who were experts in fields that I simply wasn't. Both are an essential part of becoming a successful entrepreneur.

INVESTING IN EXPERT SUPPORT

People like George are often the same people who don't believe in outsourcing. Even if they do manage to quit the rat race and start working for themselves, they get trapped in a cycle of trying to do everything themselves - partly to save money and also, potentially, because they don't believe anyone else could do it as well as them. This is a mistake. And it's the very opposite of passive income.

George and I had talked about this when he toyed with the idea of starting his own business and building a cycling app. His app development skills were rusty, so he knew he'd have to pay for help in that department. But he was shocked when I reeled off the list of support I paid for: marketing manager, copywriters to support marketing efforts, virtual assistant to help manage my time, life coach to keep me focused on my goals and mental health strategies, website manager, accountant, financial adviser, lawyers, property managers, lettings agents, mortgage broker, project managers, insurance broker. And that's before we even get to the construction teams and many consultants involved in designing a large development and bringing that design to life. These people were my dream team. My "Black Book Team" as I called them.

I certainly wasn't trying to say that George needed a team of that size for his business. But my point was, why try to do everything yourself when there are people out there who can do a better job, in less time?

'It's a wonder you make any profit,' George sniffed. 'Doesn't all that cost a fortune?'

This is most people's objection to outsourcing: the cost.

'I prefer to focus on value,' I said. 'I think to myself, is this cost worth it? Would it cost me more to do it myself?'

I explained to George an eye-opening way to determine the value of outsourcing. It starts with calculating your effective hourly rate, by taking your net income for the last six or 12 months and dividing that figure by the number of working hours.

'Say your effective hourly rate is £25 per hour,' I said to George. 'You should be outsourcing tasks that would cost less than £25 per hour, because it would cost you more to do them yourself. Say you could pay a bookkeeper £20 an hour to keep on top of your books. That's money well spent, because you doing your own bookkeeping is costing you £25 an hour! And there's a bigger cost, of course, in that you're stuck working *in* your business instead of *on* your business.'

I continued, 'If you really want to be a successful entrepreneur, you need to start thinking like a business owner. And one of the key lessons any business owner learns is that you need to be working *on* your business not *in* your business. You need to be working on growing your business and achieving your business goals, rather than handling the day-to-day minutia that keeps the business ticking along. The time you gain by outsourcing tasks to the experts is used to generate more wealth. That's why I spend my time sourcing new property sites, expanding my network, connecting with potential investors, and learning how best to leverage different forms of funding. These are all things that help take my business to the next level. If I'm stuck doing my own books or dealing with day-to-day tenant stuff, I'd never have any time left for the really important tasks. Besides, I'm aiming for as much of my income as possible to be passive. And it's not passive if I try to do everything myself.'

Bottom line, to become successful you have to surround yourself with people who support you on that journey - people who inspire you, and give you the practical support and advice you need.

YOU HAVE TWO POTS TO FILL

I like to think of it this way . . . break your skillset down into, say, 50 key skills that will help you build your path to success. For me, I'd list things like mindfulness and meditation, financial education, marketing skills, sales skills, public speaking, goal-setting, visualisation, accountancy, legal skills, writing, and presentation skills.

Even the most successful entrepreneur isn't going to be a pro at all of the skills on their list. You may only be really adept at a handful of them. But that's okay. The key to success doesn't lie in mastering all of those skills - it lies in being able to pull people into your orbit who are masters at those skills. Like a chef, combining the perfect blend of ingredients in a pot to make a bouillabaisse.

Actually, I find it easier to think of it as two pots, rather than one. The first pot is for people who inspire and motivate me, and the second is for the practical professionals who help me run and grow my business every day. For a budding property investor, I might fall into their inspirational pot because I run a mentorship programme, offer educational courses and write books that (I hope) inspire and educate people to build wealth. The same budding investor will also have a more practical pot of people who help them with their investments and business - people like estate agents, an accountant, a property solicitor, and so on.

Crucially, you can't just bung random ingredients in each pot and expect a great stew - you have to tweak the balance according to your skills and goals. A little more of one ingredient, a little less of something else. And you may find one pot needs to be much bigger than the other, which is fine.

And, once you've found your perfect blend of people, you have to keep your pots at a healthy simmer by cultivating those relationships. You don't want to let a good stew get cold! But I talk more about cultivating relationships and building rapport with people in the next chapter.

Let's explore how you can build such a support network for yourself.

FILLING YOUR INSPIRATIONAL POT

I talked a lot about the first pot of people - finding people who inspire you - back in Chapter 7. This inspiration may come in the form of a mentorship relationship, a life coach, networking with other entrepreneurs that you know in real life, or simply reading books by successful people (and/or following them on social media) and gleaning tips from their journey.

Certainly in the early days, it's often hard to get in-person access to highly successful people because they're just operating at a different level to you. (That said, such people may offer paid-for mentorship and educational opportunities, so don't rule it out entirely.) That's why I started by reading as many entrepreneurial and mindset books as I could get my hands on - I was soaking up lessons on how other successful people operated, how they spent their time, and so on, in a way that was appropriate for my level.

To be honest, that's the whole reason why I'm writing this book - because I gleaned so many success-building habits, traits and techniques just from reading what other successful people do. I wanted to distil the biggest, most eye-opening lessons for others.

But I've no doubt that having an in-person mentor would have helped me grow more rapidly in my early days. So I encourage you to find a mentor of your own - whether that's a paid-for mentorship programme, or a less formal mentorship relationship with someone you already know.

Your mentor doesn't even have to be an entrepreneur. Not necessarily. They could be a mindfulness practitioner, for example, or a life coach. Anyone who motivates you to be your best has a place in your inspirational pot. I consider my life coach to be a key ingredient in my inspirational pot because, when it comes to things like setting goals and visualising what I want, she's much smarter than me. She's much more of an expert on that topic. And she pushes me to connect deeply with my goals. So I'm not just talking about building relationships with amazing business people; I'm talking about connecting with the people who can help you fulfil your potential in general, by boosting any one of the 50-odd skills you've identified.

There may be a cost associated with working with such people. You'd have to pay for a life coach, for example. Don't shy away from paid-for relationships like this because they can deliver enormous value. In fact, it can end up creating a snowball effect.

What I mean by that is, the more you work at building relationships with inspiring people, the more inspiring people you attract to you. The law of attraction (Chapter 3) brings more inspirational people your way.

I speak from experience here, as I went from launching my own YouTube channel to co-presenting a TV programme with *Homes Under the Hammer* presenter Martin Roberts within the space of a couple of years. Martin has been on national daytime TV in the UK for over 20 years and working with him is a huge honour. It's mind-boggling, but also not, because I've been working towards becoming a leading voice in the property sector for what feels like forever, constantly seeking out people who inspire me and help me level up my career, and with whom I can create win-win relationships. So, on some level, working with Martin feels like a natural next step. Martin has been my own mentor in many ways. I love filming with him and learning presenting skills from him when we're on set. Also, by combining our various skills and contacts, Martin and I now offer high net worth clients the opportunity to joint venture (or JV) with us to share in the wealth creation that property development provides. The ultimate power team!

FILLING YOUR PROFESSIONAL POT

Dream team. Power team. Call it what you will. I like to think of it as my Black Book Team because this is the secret network of amazing professionals that help me do what I do. There's enormous value in this network, and I nurture this team like it's one of my most precious assets. Because it is. Having the right consultant on my team (a quality mortgage broker, for instance) can stop me losing a precious deal, help me get a better deal, add thousands to my bottom line, or stop me losing thousands.

This is why I consider the people I work with - and the knowledge they have - to be as valuable as my own knowledge. Maybe even more so. It's also why my mentees get direct access to my Black Book Team, my A-Team of advisers and professionals. Because I know how valuable they are, and how many years of work has gone into building such an amazing pot of people.

Who's in my Black Book Team? As my business has grown, so too has my team. It's a big pot, nowadays!

- I have my core team of people - these are the professionals I work with all the time who keep my business ticking along. Marketers, accountants, tax adviser, virtual assistant, lettings agents to find and manage tenants, and so on. This core team also includes people who help me find and assess potential property developments, and complete deals. Think property solicitor, mortgage broker, insurance broker, project manager, quantity surveyor, and so on.
- Then I have my main site team who assist with the design and build phases of pretty much every build I do. This spans contract administrators, architects, planning consultants, building surveyor, mechanical and electrical engineers, main building contractor, and so on.

- I also have project-specific consultants who may or may not be needed, depending on each project's requirements. This may include people like acoustics consultants, environmental consultants, flooding consultants, etc.

Obviously your professional pot may look very different, so don't be put off by my list. If you're keen to get into property development, a good project manager should be your first port of call. They'll help you assess sites and advise you on which professionals you do and don't need to hire.

'DO WHAT YOU DO BEST AND OUTSOURCE THE REST'

This quote by Peter Drucker sums up my approach to outsourcing. As I said in Chapter 11, to create passive income, you need to invest in technology and/or people to take care of various activities for you. Trying to do everything yourself is not very passive at all. Besides, remember that Pareto principle, or 80/20 rule, where 80% of results come from 20% of effort? You want to focus on that results-delivering 20% and let others take care of the rest.

In many areas, I'm not even the best person for the job at hand. For example, I'd be a rubbish bookkeeper and solicitor, and I don't particularly relish the day-to-day side of lettings management, so I outsource all that stuff to people that are the best in their field at those things. They'll always do a better job than I ever could.

Yes, it costs money, but it frees me up for other activities that I enjoy more or create greater value for me, such as taking a more strategic view of all my businesses and opening up higher-level opportunities. It allows me to focus on being productive, instead of busy.

And that's a really important distinction to make. Busy isn't the same as productive. I could *busy* myself all day managing tenants, and while that would keep income rolling in, it's not productive in terms of growing my business and building my wealth. We're programmed to believe that being busy is good, but it's a falsehood. This is a big mindset shift for budding entrepreneurs and, for many, it's the first obstacle to overcome on the road to passive income.

As my Rat Racer friend noted, it does cost money to outsource work to other experts. But as I explained to him, I just ask myself a simple question: would it cost me more to do it myself? In most cases, the answer is yes. Based on my hourly rate I'd be a *very* expensive lettings agent or project manager, so it makes financial sense to outsource those tasks. I use the time I gain to focus on areas of the business that will generate more wealth, such as identifying ways to grow my property portfolio.

And, of course, there are those advisers that don't just free up my time to grow my wealth - they actively make me money or save me money. A great mortgage broker, for example, can save me thousands on a big development by finding me the very best finance deal on the market. Even better, the fact that they're so deeply immersed in the mortgage market means I don't have to be.

Whatever passive income route you go down, you have to treat it like a serious business, not something you dabble in. And as with any business, it's vital you invest financially in working with the right people.

I get that it's hard to do this when money is tight or you're just starting out. It can be tough to pay out for various advisors and outsourced team members when the return may not be immediate. Paying my accountant doesn't immediately earn me money, but at the end of the year - when they (legally) save me lots of tax - their fee will have been money well spent. When money is tight, I recommend looking down your list of 50-odd skills and identifying the skills that are absolutely essential to getting your first passive income stream off the ground. That's where you should invest in the first instance.

Eventually, you may reach a point where it makes more financial sense to bring certain tasks back 'in house' and hire full-time members of staff to work for you. If the business is large and profitable enough to warrant it, and it would cost less to employ people than pay freelancers, it makes perfect sense. That's the stage I'm at now with my business, and my Black Book Team now includes a blend of freelancers and in-house employees.

HOW TO BUILD YOUR OWN BLACK BOOK TEAM

Your own team of professionals may look nothing like mine, but let me share a few thoughts on how to start building those sorts of connections.

As I mentioned, if you're considering property development, then a great project manager will help you appoint the right experts, based on each project's specific requirements. Beyond that, it doesn't matter whether you're looking for property professionals or, say, a good accountant or marketer - the principles of finding good people are the same:

- Always start with word-of-mouth recommendations from people you know. Ask your friends, colleagues and acquaintances if they've worked with a good accountant, lawyer, web developer, or whatever.
- You can also search online, check out LinkedIn and explore industry forums. But whenever you're searching for experts that haven't come via a word-of-mouth recommendation, always do your due diligence and check out their reviews.
- You can also search via the relevant accrediting bodies, where appropriate.
- Go to industry-specific networking meetings to expand your network and connect with useful contacts.
- A mentor may also be able to connect you with amazing talent. That's what I do with my property mentees - I connect them with my preferred project management firm, funders, and others in my Black Book Team.
- If possible, meet face-to-face with freelancers at least once to gauge how well you might work with them.
- Assess their experience and skill level. It's really important they have a proven track record in your desired field.

- Maybe even ask to speak to one or two of their clients for a reference. For someone like a project manager, you should also be able to visit previous sites that they've managed.
- Ask yourself, do I like this person? Can I see myself enjoying working with them? If the answer is no, even if they're highly skilled, you may be better off continuing the search. After all, in an ideal scenario, people in your Black Book Team would be working with you for many years.
- Ask yourself, does it seem like they want my business? What I mean by this is do they respond to your initial emails quickly? Do they pick up the phone when you call? If you have to work hard to get someone's attention, it doesn't bode well.

The same tips would also apply to connecting with people for your inspirational pot, such as a mentor or life coach. Word-of-mouth recommendations are always great. Be sure to do your due diligence and check out their reviews. And ask yourself whether you can work well with that person.

As time goes by - as your business grows and your own skill set evolves - the team around you will also evolve. Over the years, I've weeded out the not-so-great advisers and kept the advisers that really add value to my business. I've also upgraded to better-equipped advisers for certain areas to match the growing complexity of my business. My very first accountant just wouldn't be equipped to deal with the size of business that I run these days. It's okay to upgrade your advisers as your needs change. In fact, it's essential.

NETWORK LESSONS FROM THE RAT RACER AND THE EXTRAORDINARY MILLIONAIRE

- Someone with a Rat Racer mindset gets a kick out of being the smartest person in the room. They don't see the value in hiring someone smarter than them - in fact, they see it as a threat.
- Someone with an Extraordinary Millionaire mindset actively seeks out people who are smarter than them - people who inspire and

motivate them to do better, and practical experts who can help them run a better business every day.

- When it comes to outsourcing tasks, the Rat Racer sees only the cost.
- The Extraordinary Millionaire sees the value in outsourcing. They know it frees them up to focus on tasks that help them grow their business and achieve their goals. Besides, they know that passive income is the name of the game - and trying to do everything yourself just isn't passive.

Let's delve a little more into this notion of valuable business relationships - specifically, the importance of building rapport and creating win-win relationships.

Chapter 13

Creating Rapport and Win-Win
Relationships

'I reckon I can drive them down more than this,' George said.

My company was converting a large house into an HMO and George had asked to project manage it for me, just so he could get some hands-on experience to supplement his online education. (Yes, he had recently signed up for a course on property investment strategies and it seemed he might be finally catching the property bug.) We were sat in my yurt office looking over the detailed quote from one of my most trusted main contractors.

'I've worked with this builder before,' I said. 'They're always open to knocking the price down in return for faster payment terms. I've done it before, and saved thousands in the process. We'd need to be really sure on the cash flow, though, to make sure we can pay on quicker terms.'

George shook his head. 'No need for all that. I bet I can squeeze more out of them without giving them any better payment terms.'

'Why,' I asked, 'when we can cut a deal that works for both parties?'

'Because I like to win.'

'Say you do that,' I said. 'Let's say you drive such a hard bargain that the builder is only breaking even on the job. They'll quickly lose enthusiasm for the project. It'll become one of those frustrating projects that they just want to get done as quickly as possible, so they can move onto the next, better project. And let's say we turn up something completely unexpected in this property - like it needs a new roof or something drastic like that. How likely is the builder to work with us on finding the best solution to that problem? How likely are they to over-inflate the price for that extra work, to make up for being shafted on the rest of it? How likely are they to work with me on the next project, or the one after that?'

'I just don't want you to overpay,' George sniffed.

'I'm not. See this section here on the carpentry estimate? That's a few grand more than the other quotes we looked at, but the rest looks very competitive. You could ask them to bring the carpentry costs down in line with other firms' quotes, and negotiate an extra 10% discount for paying within, say, 21 days of completion.'

'And he'd go for that?'

'I know he will. Because I only ever work with people who are open to having these sorts of conversations. It's the same when I'm looking to buy a property.'

LOOK FOR PEOPLE, NOT JUST OPPORTUNITIES

'In fact,' I continued. 'This is one of the best tips I can give you: when you're looking for property investment opportunities, you're not just looking for the right property. You're looking for the right vendor. A vendor who's motivated to do a deal with you. Too many property investors focus only on the property. But if you find a great property that's owned by the wrong vendor, it's not going to be a good deal.'

'What do you mean by the wrong vendor?' George asked.

'When I was filming the Property Mentors TV show the other day with my friend and business partner Martin Roberts, we looked at this property in London. Prime central London location, prestigious address off Holland Park, an ex-embassy building. It'd been on the market for two years - which, in a market as rampant as the London housing market, is very telling. Yet the vendors are still chasing a price of £25 million. They think they're selling a luxury house that's ready to move into, when in reality it needs a full renovation. It's a great development opportunity, in other words, but at £25 million it's just too expensive for any developer to touch it - no one can make money on it. Which is why the vendors haven't been able to sell, despite the surging market around them. That tells me a lot about the mindset of the vendor right there. I can tell they're not open to a deal. If they were, it wouldn't still be on the market.'

'Why wouldn't they just drop the price a bit?'

'Well, because it was an embassy, it's owned by a country, isn't it? They can obviously afford to just sit on it and bide their time. They're not motivated to do a deal. So even if I was looking to splurge a lot of money on a London development, I'd look for a vendor that's actually motivated to sell.'

'So you're looking for someone who's in dire financial straits who needs to sell quickly?' George asked.

'Not necessarily, although I've found some great properties that way, by solving other people's property problems. No, I'm just looking for the kind of vendor that's willing to enter into a conversation. The kind of vendor that recognises the benefits of doing a deal with me - namely, that they'll get a realistic price and the deal will go through first time. Do you know how many vendors have come back to me after rejecting my offer? They went with a higher bid, which ultimately fell through because the buyer later realised they'd offered too much and that they'd make no money on the project. So they pull out, and the vendor is back at square one. I've seen it happen so many times.'

'So you go in with a low offer because you've done your sums and know exactly how much you need to spend on the property?'

'I go in with a *realistic* offer. Because, again, it's no benefit to me to stiff someone on the price. I want the deal to go through as much as the vendor does. If I try to cheat them by offering an unfair price, they'll pull out as soon as a better offer comes their way. And if it's a good property, rest assured a better offer will come along. Far better to agree a win-win deal that goes through first time in a timely way. Better for everyone.'

'That's all well and good,' George said. 'But when I sold my house, I remember what the estate agents were like, encouraging us to go for the highest price possible. To extract every penny we could from the property.'

'And maybe that's fine for the average house sale, where the buyer is going to just move on in and live in the house. Maybe they'll spend a bit of money doing it up, but they're not looking at it as a business opportunity. It's when you get into investment properties that you really want to buy off-market whenever you can.'

'I've been learning about this!' George's face lit up. 'Where you source properties direct, rather than going to a mainstream estate agent.'

'Exactly. If I see a commercial building that's ripe for conversion into flats, but it's up for sale with a mainstream agent, that immediately tells me that the vendor is probably looking for the highest price they can get.

That they probably don't understand - or don't want to understand - the commercial aspects of selling to a developer. That they may struggle to see that deal from both sides, where they get a realistic, fair price, and the developer can make money at their end. More often than not, when you're sourcing a development property through the main market, the numbers are probably going to be too tight. I'm not saying there's no value in working with estate agents, just that some of the best deals to be found are probably not on the open market.'

UNDERSTANDING THE OTHER PARTY'S MOTIVATIONS

'Didn't you buy this place direct from the owner?' George gestured around him at the yurt and woodland beyond the window.

He was right, my wife and I had done a deal for our dream house directly with the owner.

'Yeah, although it was originally up for sale with an estate agent. We first saw it on Rightmove and fell in love instantly. But when I called the agent, he said he was too busy to do a viewing that weekend. So we just took an innocent little drive by the house to see it from the outside.'

'I can see where this is going,' George laughed.

'Right?' I laughed with him. 'I said, "I'll just go and knock on the door and see if anyone's home." So I did, and the vendor, nice guy called John, opened the door. I did my best "sorry to bother you, but . . ." speech, explained how we'd seen the house on Rightmove and were really interested but the agent was too busy for a viewing, and how we just happened to be driving by and could we possibly arrange a viewing for a time that was convenient, please and thank you.'

'And he said . . .?'

'Of course he said, "Come on in and look around now!" So we did. We knew immediately it was the dream house. All we had to do then was convince John and his wife to sell it to us.'

'How d'you mean?' George asked. 'Didn't you just make an offer and that was it?'

'It wasn't that easy,' I explained. 'At that time, we had less than £10,000 cash sitting in the bank. And this place, including all the costs, was £1.9 million.'

George whistled.

'Exactly. With all my income-producing assets, we knew we could comfortably afford the mortgage. We just didn't have a lot of cash floating around for the deposit. And the value of our current home was about a fifth of this place, so it was a big leap on paper. I knew I was going to have to work hard to get John on my side if we were ever going to pull this deal off.'

'How'd you do it?'

'Well, like all win-win deals, it started with a conversation, with me trying to understand his position and motivations. John and his wife were in their 50s, looking to downsize. They hadn't yet bought their next place, in fact they hadn't even started looking yet because they figured it would take a long time to sell a £1.9 million property. Time was on their hands. They weren't in a rush to move on. And all the while they were talking, I was listening to their needs. We had a great chat. They liked me and my wife. We had the girls with us and I guess they just liked our family. We got to know each other a bit.'

'But the money stuff . . .' George prompted.

'Once I understood their position, and that they hadn't even started looking for their next home yet, I knew we had a chance. Before we left I asked – just straight and direct – what bottom-line figure they had in mind. Because everyone has one. Then I said we'd run the numbers and talk more in the next few days. And we did. We continued the conversation over the coming days. No estate agent involved, just John and I. And we came up with a deal where we paid their bottom-line figure, and we got a delayed completion deal – I think it was a "long-stop" completion within 12 months of exchange. So we could exchange contracts and they'd have that security of knowing the sale was 100% going through. They could look for their next home with confidence, knowing they had as much time as they needed within 12 months - no pressure to find somewhere and move by a certain date. Because I'd had that conversation with John and his wife, I knew that arrangement would work for them. And from my point of view, I was getting a fair price *and* precious time to raise the deposit funds, which was crucial to us getting this deal over the line.'

'But how on earth did you pull the money together?'

'I swung into action, obviously. I refinanced existing assets to free up some capital. Sold a couple of properties from our portfolio. Did whatever I could to get the mortgage in place. I needed to generate *a lot* of cash, as I could only arrange a £1 million mortgage. I managed to raise those hundreds of thousands within a few months of exchange, so this meant we ended up completing within just five months of me knocking on the door. That's the power of the law of attraction, big hairy goal-setting, visualisation and, of course, taking action. And, best of all, I'd freed up enough capital that we didn't even need to sell our old family home. We just switched that old mortgage to a buy-to-let mortgage to keep it. That old house pays for this house.' (See Chapter 1 for more on goal-setting, and Chapter 2 for visualisation.)

'You must be joking,' George said.

'No, really. Because we turned that house into an HMO, letting each bedroom on a separate tenancy agreement, we earn more in rental income than if we'd let it on a single tenancy agreement. And the rental income from that is enough to cover the increased mortgage payment on this place. It's like I'm always saying, if you're going to buy liabilities, do it with passive income.'

THE VALUE OF 'WIN-WIN' NOT 'I WIN, YOU LOSE'

George isn't alone in his default position of wanting to find the 'I win, you lose' scenario. Many people don't recognise the art of finding win-win relationships. In fact, many highly successful people don't value win-win scenarios. In other words, you can be successful by screwing people over left, right and centre. You can get what you want at everyone else's expense.

For someone like George, doing a deal is just a numbers game. It's about winning. In his high-powered sales career, George was all about making the sale and getting the bonus, and driving his team to do the same. If that's at the expense of the client - if the client ends up with a product or service level that's not right for them - so be it.

I could do the same thing in my property business. I could get rich renting shoddy flats to people who have no choice but to rent from me. I could drive building contractors down to the lowest possible price until they make no money working with me. I could cheat other investors out of their hard-earned money with promises of 'get rich quick' secrets.

But I don't want to be successful that way. Because I believe in the law of attraction and getting back what you give out. The only way I want to create success is by working *with* people, not against them. If I can make something work for both parties, then I will. If I can understand someone's needs and motivations, and find a way to deliver what they want - while also getting what I want - then that's what I'll do. That goes for every aspect of my business, from making sure my rental properties are high-quality places that I'd actually want to live in, to agreeing mutually beneficial terms with vendors when I buy properties. As a result, I enjoy lasting relationships and repeat business with everyone from tenants to contractors to wealthy investors.

By operating in this way, I believe I'm creating the best path to long-lasting success and abundance for me and my family. Like I said, it's not the only path. But it's the only path I want to take.

It's also important to remember that win-win isn't always about the numbers. With any business deal - whether it's buying a property, setting up a joint partnership arrangement or even just hiring a freelancer - a win-win scenario isn't always about finding a price that both parties like. The terms of the deal can be just as important as the price. In fact, this is very often where the art of the deal lies, in finding terms that are mutually beneficial.

That's how I was able to offer John, the previous owner of my dream family home, the bottom-line price that he was willing to accept. Because I could give him something that a lot of other buyers wouldn't: the flexibility to move when it suited him.

Clearly, this only works if you're dealing with someone who's actually open to communication. Someone who's willing to have a conversation, so you can understand their needs. Again, this goes for any business relationship, whether it's a client that you want to sell something to, someone you want to buy from, or someone you want to work with.

Having identified that the other party is open to having a conversation, where do you go from there?

HOW TO TURN A CONVERSATION INTO A WIN-WIN OUTCOME

My biggest tips for creating a win-win deal are:

- Build rapport with the person. Spend a little time getting to know them before you even discuss anything like price or terms. I'm not saying you must ask for their life story, just a brief and light conversation, nothing heavy. That's all it took before John and I started talking about the money stuff - a brief chat as we looked around the house and garden.
- Listen. I can't stress this enough, active listening is a key part of finding win-win scenarios. Really listen to what they're saying, don't just wait for them to stop talking so you can get your point across. Only by listening can you glean info on their needs and motivations.
- Put yourself in their shoes and consider what external factors may be affecting their decision. For example, do they have children? Have they inherited this property? Are they having a tough time health wise? Do they need a quick outcome? How much do they need the money? By listening and building rapport, you can extract this sort of information in the course of a polite conversation, without ever

having to ask for it directly. You can understand what sort of factors may be motivating them based on what they say.

- Now ask yourself, what's their biggest problem here? Is it time, money, uncertainty, stress, or something else altogether? Then ask yourself how you can create a solution to that problem.

- Emphasise your credentials and experience. As I mentioned, I've had a lot of vendors come back to me after another developer has over-offered and later pulled out of the deal. So when I'm making an offer on a site or property, I emphasise my ability to get the deal done first time. I know my numbers, and I know my offer is realistic - both in terms of the vendor getting a good price and there being future profit left on the table for me. Very often, this security is enough to bring wavering vendors over to my side.

- Keep the lines of communication open. It's doubtful you'll reach an agreement within the space of one conversation. So, having built that initial rapport, work at maintaining it. Keep in touch and keep the friendly conversation going. For example, after we had our spur-of-the-moment viewing, I followed up later that day to thank John and his wife for their time and to confirm that we'd be in touch soon.

- Set expectations. Just as you want to understand the other party's needs, be clear about your own. Do you need an answer by a certain date, for example? Do you need two weeks to get your finance ducks in a row before you can get back to them? Then say so. Don't overpromise and underdeliver.

- Build and maintain trust. This one's easy - do what you say you're going to do.

- And show your appreciation. When they do what they said they would do, say thank you. When they say they'll consider your offer, say thank you. Give recognition and make sure they feel valued in the conversation.

CREATING THAT FEELING OF INSTANT RAPPORT

Let's dwell on the notion of rapport. Because I'm certain that rapport played a big role in securing the home of my dreams when my wife and

I weren't remotely in the position to buy it (at least, not based on the money we had in the bank). At the end of the day, the vendors liked me and my family. We bonded over a shared love of nature and the local area of outstanding natural beauty. That initial rapport was enough for us to further the conversation. If the vendors hadn't taken a shine to us, they could have shut the conversation down by saying they weren't looking for offers below the asking price.

Rapport is an important skill, and like any skill it can be learned. Sure, it comes more naturally to some people than others, but anyone can learn to build rapport.

I'm lucky in that I learned how to build rapport by watching how my dad talked to people. He could connect with anyone. Whenever he'd go to the rubbish tip, my brother and I would beg to go along so we could rummage through the bric-a-brac bits for sale. (Much to my mum's frustration, we usually came home with as much stuff as we'd offloaded at the tip!) I loved looking at the old bikes and toys and picking a few things to take home, but I also loved watching my dad negotiate with the men who worked at the tip. I noticed that he'd change his language to match theirs, and mirror their body language. There would be a bit of chit-chat, a couple of laughs about something or other, or maybe a commiseration (football, the weather, how busy it was at the tip, anything). Then my dad would casually ask 'How much for this, then?' He'd knock a few quid off the quoted price, and invariably, the other guy would accept. I was always watching, and I really admired how my dad could get on with anyone. I've no doubt if he'd ever met the Queen, he'd have been talking about horses and corgis and handbags within seconds.

And it's not as though he was being fake. He just knew how to connect with people. I like to think that's rubbed off on me. I always look to connect with people in a genuine way, especially in those all-important first moments, when we're forming an impression of each other.

By building rapport with people, I can get into their head more easily. I don't mean that in a creepy way. I just mean it helps me understand what they really want, so that I can find a way to make that happen, while also getting what I want.

If you feel like rapport doesn't come naturally to you, don't despair. Treat it as another skill that you can develop through continual education, just as you can learn about meditation and visualisation and passive income streams. Seek out books and courses that help you connect with people. Work on memory techniques, so you can better remember people's names and little titbits about them. Learn communication techniques that help you communicate in a clear and engaging way. Pay attention to your own and other people's body language so you can a) put them at ease by adopting a relaxed posture yourself, and b) mirror their own gestures.

SEEKING OUT THE DIRECT DEALS

One of the best ways to find win-win opportunities, especially when it comes to property, is to seek out deals before they hit the open market. So, when I'm looking for investment properties, I'm not trawling websites for the latest listings. I'm sourcing off-market as much as I can, seeking out properties *before* they're advertised for sale.

Now, if you're not interested in investing in property, feel free to skip this section. But I wanted to briefly talk about the merits of off-market sourcing because it's a great way to get ahead of competing investors. And if you can be one step ahead of the competition, you generally have a little more leeway to negotiate those win-win outcomes, move quickly and avoid being outbid.

Again, I'm not averse to working with estate agents and sourcing agents. Far from it. If someone finds a great site that I haven't found myself, I absolutely want to know about it, and I'm happy to pay a finder's fee or commission in return. And I make damn sure estate agents and sourcing agents know exactly what sort of property lights my fire, so when the right property comes across their books, I'm the first person they call.

It's just that most of the best deals of my career have come from direct conversations with vendors. This means I'll frequently approach property owners and landowners directly, or encourage them to come to me.

If you're serious about finding win-win property deals, I highly recommend you:

- Scout your target area and identify sites that suit your specific property strategy (HMO, serviced accommodation, etc.), then approach the owner directly to see if they might be interested in selling up. You can drop off a letter or flyer, for example, or do what I did and knock on the door.
- If lots of local properties fit your bill, narrow down your options to those where the owner is more likely to be motivated to sell. With the exception of that embassy building in London, vacant buildings are usually a great example.
- Encourage owners to approach you directly, by sending out letters or flyers saying that you're a private investor looking for sites to develop (be clear on which types of property or land you're looking for).
- You might even invest in online, social media or local newspaper ads targeting owners in a specific area.
- Spread the word among your network, including building contractors, architects, your solicitor, etc. They may know of people in their own network who might be thinking of selling up. You could always offer a finder's fee for introductions that lead to a successful purchase.
- There are also lots of online sourcing tools popping up these days which help you target potential deals. They look through land registry searches and planning portal updates, amongst other things, to help you target your next property deal.

As per my tips from earlier in the chapter, when you're approaching people directly, it's really important to build rapport, listen, and try to understand their motivations and needs. And do be sure to stress the benefits of selling directly to you, i.e. a quick sale, at a fair price and with no agent's commission.

BUILDING WIN-WIN RELATIONSHIPS WITH YOUR BLACK BOOK TEAM

In Chapter 12, we looked at the importance of outsourcing and building a team of people around you who are more expert at various tasks than your good self. Once you've found these people, and assuming you like how they operate, it's vital you keep them happy. Since outsourcing is such a key part of passive income, I thought I'd give a few tips on keeping your dream team of freelancers, consultants and experts happy. But really, these tips can be applied to anyone you do business with.

Keeping people happy makes for a better working relationship, but it'll also make it easier to connect with other experts in future. If you're a great client to work with, your solicitor will be much more comfortable referring you to a tax adviser they know and trust, and so on. If you're a nightmare to work with - screwing people over left, right and centre - you can forget about referrals.

To make sure people want to keep working with you:

- Pay people on time. You don't have to pay early. But pay on time.
- Keep in touch regularly. This builds rapport, and ensures projects run more smoothly. I talk to my project manager almost daily when we're collaborating on a project. And even if I'm not currently working with someone (for example, an estate agent), I might still drop them an occasional email asking how they are and if they have any good properties coming onto the market soon.
- Be very clear about your expectations. Always agree (preferably in writing) what work you need doing, and to what standard.
- Review your arrangement regularly, ideally every six months but at least once a year. This doesn't need to be anything too formal - just a chat about how the arrangement is going and whether anything could be done to make things run more smoothly.
- Treat other people's time as carefully as your own. Which means don't waste their time, or call them on a Sunday morning, or email them with an 'Urgent' subject line when you know they're on holiday.

- Pay it forward by recommending your Black Book folks to others in your network. Providing there's no conflict of interest, why shouldn't you recommend your amazing contacts to other people you know? Remember, referrals work both ways, so if you recommend someone, they'll be more inclined to do the same for you.
- Give credit where credit's due. Everyone likes to hear that they're doing a good job, so say thank you for a job well done and express how much you appreciate their work.

BUSINESS RELATIONSHIP LESSONS FROM THE RAT RACER AND THE EXTRAORDINARY MILLIONAIRE

- Someone with a Rat Racer mindset may not see the value in creating win-win business relationships and outcomes. They're happy with 'I win, you lose' scenarios.
- Someone with an Extraordinary Millionaire mindset seeks outcomes where both parties benefit in some way. This may be a price that works for both parties – but it can equally be about finding mutually beneficial terms. The Extraordinary Millionaire knows that win-win outcomes are good for business because they lead to long-lasting relationships and repeat custom.
- The Rat Racer looks for opportunities, not people.
- The Extraordinary Millionaire looks to do business with people who are open to having a conversation and finding a mutually beneficial way forward. So when it comes to potential property investments, they're looking as much for the right vendor as they are for the right property.
- In any deal or agreement, a Rat Racer will focus on their own motivations and desires.
- An Extraordinary Millionaire knows that understanding the other party's situation, needs and motivations sows the seeds for a win-win outcome.
- The Rat Racer underestimates the importance of rapport and listening.

- The Extraordinary Millionaire knows that by building rapport and listening, you can better understand the other party's needs. Rapport and listening are fundamental to gaining and building long-lasting business relationships.
- Someone with a Rat Racer mindset may think 'I'm not a people person' and leave it at that.
- Someone with an Extraordinary Millionaire mindset knows that rapport is a skill, and like any skill, it can be learned or improved.

Win-win relationships and outcomes are great, but when you're an entrepreneur, not everything is going to go your way. A key part of success, therefore, is learning to not fear failure. Which brings us to the next tool in the Extraordinary Millionaire toolkit . . .

Chapter 14

Getting Comfortable with Failure

'I think I'm turning into you,' George said.

'Oh yeah, how so?' I asked.

'A friend at work is leaving to start a rival software business. She told me she's ploughed all her savings into starting the business.'

'Sounds risky.'

'That's exactly what I thought,' George said. 'All I could think was how she'd be better off building her business as a side gig first, or building more of a buffer by investing in income-producing assets before she jumped ship. Then, if the business ultimately fails - which, let's be honest, a lot of them do - she won't have lost everything. She's thinking how I used to think a few years ago. It really showed me how far I've come, you know, mindset-wise. These days, I wouldn't dream of just jumping ship like that. I'm building my passive income buffer first.'

After project managing a couple of my HMO conversions, and doing some courses on property strategies, George was taking his own small steps into property investing. Short on capital, he was going down a rent-to-rent route, renting a house and subletting it as an HMO. After paying the rent and bills, he was left with a £500 profit each month - for very little work.

'And once you've built up a healthy buffer,' I said, 'you can escape the rat race in a less risky fashion. You'll be free to try various things and learn what works and what doesn't. You can afford to fail, because you won't lose everything.'

WHY IT'S OKAY TO FAIL

'Actually,' I continued, 'I don't even like that word fail. Providing you leave the rat race in a smart way - i.e. not ploughing your life savings into one business - there's no such thing as failure. Some things may not work out, but those are just learning opportunities. In my mind, you're either making money or you're learning. Those are the only two settings. If you're learning, you're not failing.'

'Yeah, but that's easy for you to say when everything you touch turns to gold,' George said.

'No it doesn't!' I protested. 'On a micro level, I'm failing all the time. On every property I develop, there's always something that I could have done better or more efficiently. That's okay. I learn from those things. And on a bigger level, I've had entire businesses fail.'

'You have?'

'Of course. I've had a number of startups over the years and they haven't all worked out. Back in 2008, when the financial crisis hit and property sales fell off a cliff, I started a sustainability consultancy, advising businesses on energy-saving measures. It was a great business idea, but I was five years too early. People just weren't as interested in green policies at that time. Now of course it's totally different, but back then the market wasn't ready.'

'So the business folded?'

'Yeah, I shut it down about nine months after starting and moved on. Financially I was fine because I had rental income coming in every month, so I wasn't worried about losing everything. I could afford to take a chance. That's the thing about building multiple streams of passive income - they may not all be wild successes, but because you've got that diversity of income, you have more security.'

'It's funny hearing you talk about having security, when that's supposedly the main selling point of staying in the rat race,' George said. 'That's why it's so hard to break out of the rat race, because we're afraid of losing what we have. The house. Savings. If my friend's business fails, what will she do then? She'll end up back in the rat race, but worse off than before. I mean, I admire her guts, taking the leap. But that fear of losing everything is what keeps most people staying in their "secure" jobs.' George made air quotes with his fingers. 'The worst thing is, it's not even real security. I could lose my job at any time. My company made 20 people redundant last week. My department was spared, but who knows for how long. I'm glad I'm building my own route out. I just wish I'd started years ago. You had the right idea, starting in your early twenties.'

'Thinking about it, I started way before then. Even when I was a kid, I was always cooking up entrepreneurial schemes. Selling sherbet to my school friends. Selling cherries on the street. One summer my brother and I sold the koi carp out of our parents' pond!'

'You never,' George laughed.

'We did. The carp had got out of control and there were way too many for the size of pond. So we started selling them to neighbours and passers-by. Then we figured out we could sell them by the bucket-load to the local garden centre. We made £100 per bucket!'

'And your parents didn't mind?'

'Mum drove us to the garden centre! With buckets of fish sloshing around in the car. She just wanted rid of them, I think. Anyway, it was a good scheme. We made a few hundred quid on that one. They were happy to support our little business ideas, Mum and Dad. That's why I'm always encouraging my kids to be entrepreneurial. To get out there and try business ventures as early as possible in life.'

'Before they have all the liabilities that come later in life,' George added.

'Exactly. And if they fail, that's fine. Failing early in life is no bad thing because they'll be learning what works and what doesn't. We give them the freedom to fail in all sorts of areas. Which is why we let them roam the woodland and we don't helicopter over them. If they fall over and hurt themselves, they'll learn. With the older two, now that they're old enough to have a lot of homework, we let them take responsibility for all that. We don't stand over them to make sure they do their homework or revise for their tests. We expect them to do it for themselves. And if they don't, well, they'll get in trouble at school won't they? And they'll learn from that too.'

'God, my sister practically does my nephew's revision for him,' George said. 'It's a whole thing, every weekend, where they sit there and do it together. He's coming up on his mock GCSEs for crying out loud. He's old enough to do it for himself. I've tried hinting that it's not exactly benefitting him, but what can you do?'

'But what's the worst that would happen if he was left to his own devices?' I asked. 'He'd fail his mock GCSEs and it'd probably be a kick up the bum to revise better for the real thing. Even if he failed his actual GCSEs, there's always the option of retaking them. I find the whole mindset of avoiding failure at any cost really odd. In my experience, really successful people are successful not because they never get anything wrong, but because they're so good at overcoming failure. They just move on and create more successful businesses. Look at Richard Branson. The Virgin Group has had, what, 14 or 15 businesses fail.'

'That many?' George asked.

'Remember Virgin Cola?'

'No . . .'

'Exactly! But overall the Virgin Group has been enormously successful. For someone like Richard Branson, failure isn't an ending, it's just part of the process. It's like Winston Churchill said, "Success is not final, failure is not fatal. It is the courage to continue that counts."'

'I like that,' George said. 'Failure is not fatal. I'll have to keep that one in mind.'

'It helps though, if you can learn to fail fast, rather then keep flogging a dead horse, as the saying goes.'

'Like your eco business?'

I nodded. 'I could easily have kept plugging away at it for years and years until the market caught up and it eventually became a success. But I wanted to grow my income and that business wasn't serving that goal, so I pulled the plug early and refocused on learning more property strategies instead. It's a whole business ethos, failing fast.'

'I hear about it all the time in the tech world,' George said. 'Fail fast, fail often.'

'Well, I prefer fail fast, fail early. But yeah, I get what they mean. You want to have the freedom to fail, but in a way that each failure helps you be more successful next time.'

'But how fast is failing fast?' George asked. 'You gave that eco business nine months. Is that a good rule of thumb for trying new businesses or investment strategies?'

'I don't know that there is a rule of thumb,' I admitted. 'It depends on things like your cash flow, amount of passive income, and factors like that. I'd also base it on feedback from clients and leads and others in the industry. If everyone's telling you that they're not ready to invest in sustainability measures - which is what we were hearing a lot of back in 2008 - then that's clearly a sign that I need to either shut the business or change what it does. Try a different offering or business model or something like that. You have to listen to what the market is telling you. More than that, if you're going to fail fast and go on to have more success, you have to actually learn how to fail.'

LEARNING TO FAIL

As I said to George, successful people don't avoid failure. They just know how to get back up and thrive despite things not going their way. In other words, they know *how* to fail. And learning how to fail is a skill that will benefit every budding entrepreneur.

The best thing you can do for yourself is to develop what psychologist and bestselling author Carol Dweck calls the 'growth mindset'. (I highly recommend her book *Mindset*.) Someone with a growth mindset sees failures and setbacks as just another milestone on the road to achieving their goals. Failures are just opportunities to learn and improve.

In contrast, someone with a 'fixed mindset' will avoid challenges to avoid failing in the first place. Which is why so many people end up in the rat race for life - because they don't want to take the risk of failing as an entrepreneur. And when they do encounter failure or setbacks, someone with a fixed mindset will believe it's because their talents and traits are fixed. So if they fail at something, rather than seeing it as a learning opportunity, they're more likely to think, 'Oh, I'm just not suited to this. It's not for me.' And they give up.

If you lean more towards the fixed mindset, don't worry. It's just a way of thinking and, as the law of attraction teaches us, thoughts can always be changed. You can learn to adopt a growth mindset. It's a conscious choice.

As well as learning more about the growth mindset, and how to adopt it, here are some other ways you can learn to fail like the best of 'em:

- **Don't be so hard on yourself.** Research has shown that women are especially prone to blaming their own flaws when things go wrong (men, on the other hand, are more likely to point the finger at external factors). I'm not saying you shouldn't take a good look at how you could do things better next time - that's obviously helpful. Just don't think, 'I'm inherently flawed. I can't do this. I shouldn't take risks like this again.'
- **Remind yourself of all the things you get right.** In times of failure, it can be hard to remember that we also get plenty of things right. In other words, you are not the sum total of your failure! A big reason successful people bounce back so well from failure is because they *believe* they're successful, even when they're not. The tools from Part I of this book can be really helpful here, especially positive affirmations.
- **If you avoid challenges because you fear failure, ask yourself, 'What's the worst that might happen if I fail at this?'** And crucially, 'What will I do if the worst does happen? How will I deal with it and move forward in a positive way?'
- **Practise taking risks.** The old advice to 'do one thing every day that scares you' may sound extreme, but it's actually pretty good advice. I'm not talking about skydiving or putting yourself in the way of physical harm - more, low-stakes things that make you nervous. Public speaking is a good one for me. I used to avoid speaking in front of audiences because it made me nervous. And, to be honest, it still does a bit. But I worked at it and worked at it until I can now present a TV show with confidence. How could you practise being outside of your comfort zone in small ways? You could, for example, try your hand at haggling on a price, or complain when you receive poor service (instead of just letting it slide for an easy life), or try a new physical activity, like horse riding.

Another great thing you can do is to work on your adaptability. I believe the best businesses are run by creative, adaptable people who have the ability to pivot and do things differently when they fail. (Brings to mind that old saying 'Insanity is doing the same thing over and over again and expecting a different result.')

Becoming a lifelong learner will help you immensely here as that's all about continual self-improvement (which, again, feeds into that growth mindset). But here are some other tips to build your adaptability muscles:

- **When it comes to passive income streams and business ventures, don't rely on one idea to see you through.** Security comes from having diversity of income streams - whether that's multiple passive income strategies or a business that has multiple sources of revenue. This is how I was able to survive huge obstacles like the financial crisis and coronavirus pandemic - because I'm never reliant on one single source of income. So if property sales stagnate, as they did during the financial crisis and the early days of the pandemic, my rental income will see me through comfortably. And should the rental market take a nosedive, I have developments that I can sell.
- **Work on your problem-solving abilities.** Problem-solving can seem like a vague skill that you either have or haven't, but in fact it's just about following a problem-solving framework: first you identify the problem, then you outline potential solutions, then you identify the best solution from the multiple options available, and finally you put that solution into motion. Practise these steps with everyday problems and you'll be more confident at solving bigger life and business problems.
- **Be more mindful.** Too often we jump in with a quick solution or try to control everything that's going on around us, when sometimes it's better to just pause. This is where mindfulness can be really useful because it teaches us to be present - as opposed to dwelling on what's happened (which cannot be changed) or worrying about what may happen next. It also allows us to reflect on what's going on around us without judgement. Without trying to control the things we can't. Without letting emotions take over. In other words, it can help you 'lean into' whatever is going on and approach situations

more objectively. And this will help to improve your judgement and problem solving.

- **Get comfortable with change.** After all, change is the only constant in life. Practising being outside of your comfort zone will certainly help you cope with change. But also try to focus on the positive benefits of any change – big or small – as opposed to focusing on the aspects that you don't like.

Finally, the biggest tip I can give you is to start doing these things now, *before* you quit the rat race. Don't wait until you actually become an entrepreneur before you start thinking and acting like one. Learn these skills now so that you have the ability to better roll with the punches when you do leave the rat race behind. It's like the law of attraction teaches us, if you think and act like an adaptable person who can bounce back from adversity, that is ultimately what you'll become.

FAILURE LESSONS FROM THE RAT RACER AND THE EXTRAORDINARY MILLIONAIRE

- Someone with a Rat Racer mindset may avoid taking risks because they fear failure.
- Someone with an Extraordinary Millionaire mindset knows that failure is just another step on the path to success.
- The Rat Racer is prone to thinking successful people never face adversity.
- The Extraordinary Millionaire knows that successful people aren't successful because they never get anything wrong – they just know how to fail. They're not defined by their failures. They use failures to inform their future successes.
- A Rat Racer may be more prone to fixed mindset thinking – where you can either do something or you can't. Therefore, a failure shows that they're not cut out for something.
- Whereas an Extraordinary Millionaire has a growth mindset. As such, they know that failures and setbacks are just opportunities to learn and improve.

- The Rat Racer doesn't see failure as something you can learn to do well.
- The Extraordinary Millionaire knows that anyone can learn to cope with failure and adversity in a better way.
- The Rat Racer may put all their eggs in one basket, which is a risky way to fail.
- The Extraordinary Millionaire has multiple streams of income, and this allows them to try new things - and to fail at some of them without losing everything.
- The Rat Racer may struggle with adaptability.
- The Extraordinary Millionaire constantly works to become more adaptable. They push themselves outside of their comfort zone in regular, even small ways. They do this even before they leave the rat race, to prepare themselves for life as a successful, adaptable entrepreneur.

Fear of failure can stem from many sources, such as the fact that we're conditioned to think the rat race is more secure than being an entrepreneur (when in reality that's not true). But it can also stem from a lack of confidence and self-belief. So let's explore confidence in a little more detail and see how anyone can learn to be more confident in life and business.

Chapter 15

Having the Confidence to Take the Leap

It was a day for celebrations. Our Rat Racer friend and his wife had just exchanged on their first ever investment property, an investment-earning personal asset to complement the rent-to-rent portfolio that he'd been steadily building. George had calculated that if he carried on with his property education and building his passive income streams, he would be able to leave the rat race behind within the next three years. He was well on his way to becoming an Extraordinary Millionaire. And I was thrilled for him. My wife and I had organised a celebratory party in our garden to mark the occasion.

In my family, we'd also achieved a (small, but fun) milestone of our own – we'd finally erected the zip line I'd been promising my kids for years. Since long before we bought our dream home. This was the first day we'd had guests over since the zip line had gone up and it was a joy to see the kids and their friends going wild on it.

HAVING THE (WELL-PLACED) CONFIDENCE TO BREAK OUT OF SOCIETY'S MOULD

'It takes a lot of confidence to go on this journey,' I said to George. 'But you're doing it. Congratulations.'

'Yeah,' George sighed. 'I'm finally making the leap into the unknown.'

'Don't do yourself an injustice,' I corrected him. 'You're not leaping into the unknown. You're acting with calculated confidence, not blind stupidity. You can be confident that you'll leave the rat race behind for good because you're laying the groundwork and building your passive income. You didn't just ditch your job and go for it like you dreamed of when I first met you. You got some education and training under your belt. You're not leaping into the unknown at all. You're making a strategic and calculated step into the next phase of your life.'

'True,' George nodded. 'I need to remind myself of that sometimes.'

'Now, on paper, what I did was a risky leap, quitting my well-paying job to live on £500 a month passive income. But even that small safety net was enough to give me confidence. Mind you, I was young and didn't have the same sort of liabilities and responsibilities that we have now. The older you get and the more liabilities you have, the higher the risk.'

'Which is what keeps people like me in the rat race,' George said. 'You think to yourself, "Oh, I'll just wait until we've paid that off, or paid this other thing off." Meanwhile, you buy a bigger house or get a new car and the liabilities grow. Because what hard-working 40-year-old doesn't want to upgrade their car every few years or live in a nice home? We want to be rewarded for putting up with life in the rat race. But that only keeps us locked into the rat race for even longer.'

'Makes me think of the Sirens in Greek mythology,' I said, 'tempting sailors towards the shore with the sweetness of their voices. Only for the boats to crash on the rocks.'

'Exactly,' George laughed. 'The rat race is a bloody Siren call, tempting people to take on more liabilities because "go on, you deserve it". We're just helpless sailors, hypnotised by its song.'

'Well, not me,' I laughed. 'And not you either, now. That tempting Siren song is exactly why people need to build their confidence before they quit the rat race, by doing what you've done: education, training, continual improvement, learning various passive income strategies, and, crucially, learning to pay for liabilities with passive income. That's a big part of having the confidence to finally leave the rat race. When you know that your liabilities are covered and you won't end up broke and homeless, or shipwrecked on the rocks of life to continue the analogy. That's the kind of confidence that only comes from knowing the mortgage is taken care of each month.'

CHOOSING EDUCATION OVER ENTERTAINMENT

George shook his head, almost in wonder. 'It feels like unlocking some kind of secret life hack, to be honest. I don't know why everyone isn't doing this.'

'Oh I suspect most people would quit the rat race tomorrow if there was an easy, overnight way to make it happen. People are always asking me for my biggest tip for becoming a property millionaire, and when I tell them it's education, they almost always look disappointed. It sounds harsh, but the fact that they have to spend time educating themselves puts the majority of people off.'

'You think?' George asked.

I nodded. 'It's like Jay Shetty always says, "Successful people prioritise education over entertainment." Most people who end up stuck in the rat race forever spend their spare time entertaining themselves when they should be educating themselves. Now, I like fishing and movies and tinkering away on the guitar as much as the next bloke, but I make damn sure I work on my continual improvement as well.'

'You're right,' George said. 'Things only really changed for me when I finally accepted that I needed to invest in my education - and I mean time as well as money. Before then, I'd spend hours every night crashing out in front of crap TV when I could have been spending at least some of that time reading a book or watching an educational video on YouTube. If I'd spent my time better a decade ago, I'd already be out of the rat race.'

'True, but back then you weren't as connected to your goals and your passion as you are now. You wanted to create an app - and maybe you still will one day - and you wanted to not have to go to work every day. You had a dream but not a passion. It's different now. I can see you're passionate about making this work. You've lit a fire in your belly. "To succeed you have to believe in something with such a passion that it becomes a reality." Anita Roddick said that. And she knew a thing or two about becoming successful.'

'Well, I'll drink to that,' George said. 'To confidence and passion–'

There was a shriek of wild joy from the direction of the zip line.

'–and whizzing down zip lines,' I finished George's toast for him.

INSTILLING THAT CONFIDENCE IN THE NEXT GENERATION

George eyed the zip line with obvious suspicion. He'd been apprehensive about letting his kids go on the zip line and only his oldest child was allowed to have a go.

'I don't want you going on that,' I'd heard him say earlier to his middle child, who was nearly old enough to leave primary school. 'You might get hurt.'

And this from a guy who had, in his youth, solo-cycled across Europe with nothing but a tent and a few Euros to his name!

I'd pointed out that the zip line had been built by professionals (and was a far cry from the rickety affair I'd erected as a kid). And that there were younger kids getting on it just fine. But the damage was done. I could see the little girl was no longer quite so keen to have a go. She headed for the swing instead and watched the zip lining crew from below.

Meanwhile, as we'd been enjoying our conversation about escaping the Siren call of the rat race, George's youngest child, who was coming up on her sixth birthday, had been clinging to her mother and wouldn't leave the patio area.

Eventually, I called one of my daughters over. 'Why don't you ask Lily if she wants to go and pick some flowers?' I prompted her.

'I already tried,' my daughter replied. 'But she doesn't want to. She only wants to stay here with the grown-ups.'

So I tried offering a lifeline to Lily's mother, George's wife. 'Would she like to see the treehouse?' I nodded at the little girl. 'Skyla will take her. She'll keep an eye on her.'

'She's okay here, thanks,' came the reply.

George shrugged at me in that resigned way that says this sort of thing happened all the time. 'She's shy. She's not great in new situations.'

I'd never tell a friend how to parent their child, but it struck me as odd that a confident person like George would raise his kids to be anything but confident. George was taking (albeit calculated) risks with his property investing, yet he was teaching his children to be risk averse. To only stay within their comfort zone.

If my children had a clingy moment (all kids do at some time or other) when we were entertaining friends, I'd gently tell them that we were having some adult time and it was time for them to go off and play. But then, my wife and I had always encouraged our children to interact with other kids they didn't know, at birthday parties and so on, and even to talk to adults with confidence. All of our children were happy to approach a waiter in a restaurant, for example, and ask where the toilets were or order another drink for themselves. Even our four-year-old would order for himself when we were eating out - much to the surprise of waiters, who were used to directing their attention at parents.

Bottom line, we made a conscious effort not to helicopter over our children at all times or do everything for them. But it's hard to tell another parent that even though they're acting out of love, they may not be acting in their child's best interest in that moment.

If that sounds judgmental, let me put it this way: one of the very best things about having the confidence to change your life and chart a brave new course for yourself is passing that same wonderful gift onto your children. So they too have the confidence to break out of society's mould and decide how to live life their way. I would have loved to see George and his wife enjoy that blessing, and maybe they would in time. George was, after all, still in the early stages of his Extraordinary Millionaire journey. Over time, I hoped he'd begin to pass the lessons he was learning - things like setting goals, being passionate about something, going after what you want, taking (calculated) risks and believing in yourself - onto his family. Time would tell.

But let's leave George and his young family at this point in their journey and turn to you, reader. What's your relationship with confidence?

DEFINING CONFIDENCE

To be clear, confidence isn't quitting your job tomorrow and sticking two fingers up at the rat race when you don't have any sort of financial buffer or passive income. That's not confidence, that's recklessness.

So what exactly is confidence? Confidence is self-belief. To be confident is to *believe* in your ability to achieve the things you want or navigate certain situations. And it's not always a hard-and-fast thing. I used to be super-confident at meeting people and making a great impression in a face-to-face scenario, but put me in front of a camera or an audience and I'd feel like jelly. I've since learned to build my confidence in that area – and we'll get to confidence-building techniques later in the chapter.

Confidence is important because it boosts success. I've talked about the law of attraction many times in this book and the importance of thinking like a successful person. It's hard to do that if you fundamentally lack confidence in your own abilities. You can repeat positive affirmations like 'I am successful' or 'Money flows to me' until you're blue in the face. But you're wasting your time if the voice in your head responds 'Yeah, but really, you suck. You're never going to achieve anything.'

This is precisely why people who are more confident do well academically (a scientific link, by the way). Because they believe they'll do well. Their internal voice is telling them they can do it.

Confidence is also closely linked to motivation, and lack of confidence can sap motivation like a vampire. It's hard to be motivated to get up every day and make time for your positive affirmations, visualisation, meditation, self-care and education when deep down you feel it's never going to lead to anything. Therefore, lack of self-belief may be the reason why so many people fall off the self-improvement wagon.

Let me also stress that a confident person isn't someone who rides roughshod over everyone else who stands in their way. Confidence isn't about achieving what you want at the expense of those around you. Far from it. To be truly confident is to celebrate other people's success, rather than feeling threatened by them. Which again brings us back to the law of attraction and that notion of getting back what we put out there. If you're a positive, optimistic person – someone who raises the confidence of those around them and encourages them to fulfil their potential, and celebrates with them when they do – you're also feeding into your own confidence and success at the same time.

CONFIDENCE-BUILDING TECHNIQUES

Sure, some people are generally more confident than others, but we can all work to build confidence. It's a skill, just like learning to ride a bike or speak another language.

The mindset techniques from Part I of this book will help you to build confidence, especially visualisation (great for mentally preparing yourself for specific situations, by visualising it going well), positive affirmations (great for boosting positivity and overall self-belief), and mindfulness (great for dealing with overwhelm or for when you feel nervous about something that may or may not happen).

Here are some other tips for boosting your self-confidence:

- **Surround yourself with people who lift you up.** By which I mean confident, optimistic people, as opposed to people who drag you down. If you find yourself feeling bummed out after spending time with someone, ask yourself whether it's really worth continuing with that relationship.
- **Don't compare yourself to others.** One scientific study found a clear link between envy – which stems from comparing ourselves to others – and how we feel about ourselves. The more envy people experienced, the worse they thought of themselves. So when you find yourself making comparisons – so-and-so has a better house, is more successful, is more confident – try to remember that comparisons don't serve you. The only competition is with yourself. Even in business, I'm not looking at what my competitors are doing. I'm looking at my goals, what I want out of life, and how I'm going to get there. Try to do the same.

- **Look after yourself.** Mentally, physically, even spiritually (if that matters to you). Habits like eating a healthy diet, exercising regularly and practising meditation have a proven relationship with confidence. It makes sense when you think about it; it's hard to feel positive and confident when you're knackered, hungover, have binged on junk food and haven't left the house all weekend!
- **Admit when you're wrong and learn to laugh at yourself.** Confident people don't think they're perfect. They have the courage to see themselves as they are and the humility to accept themselves, warts and all. That's true confidence.
- **Remind yourself that it's okay to try and fail.** It's all part of learning and becoming successful. Circle back to Chapter 14 for more on this.
- **Be open-minded to new situations and experiences.** Stepping outside of your comfort zone can do wonders for your self-esteem. Again, there's more on building your adaptability back in Chapter 14.

CONFIDENCE IN RELATION TO LEAVING THE RAT RACE

Clearly confidence plays a big role in becoming an Extraordinary Millionaire because, as I said to George, it takes guts to break out of the 'normal' path that we're all led to believe is right. You know, you must go to college or university, get a good job, work your way up, save your pennies, cling onto that supposed security at all costs. Saying 'no thanks, I think I'll try a different way' is brave as hell. You can't do it without self-belief.

And you'll no doubt encounter people who'll - without even meaning to - try to dent that self-confidence. People might tell you you're mad. That it's too risky. Your parents, friends, maybe even your spouse. George's wife was certainly nervous about him getting into property. But that nervousness came from a place of not being informed about passive income. Because George had educated himself, he knew with confidence that what he was doing was actually less risky than thinking he could stay in the same career for the next thirty years of his working life. In this age of rapid and vast change, the days of a job for life are long gone. The 'security' of the rat race is just a myth.

That naysaying 'don't do it' voice may even be coming from inside your own head. But very often that little voice in our head is an echo of other people's voices.

You love these people - yourself included, I hope - but that doesn't mean you have to listen to them. Allow yourself to believe in a different message: 'I can and I will'. Whenever someone tells you you can't, imagine their words written on a piece of paper and visualise that piece of paper catching fire. That fire is fuel for your passion. Every time someone ever told me I couldn't do something - even when that message came from a place of love or light-hearted joking among mates - it only drove me on to prove them wrong.

That said, I've always acted with calculated confidence in mind. Sure, it may have looked nutty when I quit my job and I only had £500 a month in passive income. But at the time my outgoings were covered by rental income, I was effectively mortgage-free, and I didn't have any family responsibilities. The risk, as I saw it, was small. Especially as I knew I was embarking on a mission of education and training. Just £500 a month was a small start, but that little bit of passive income boosted my confidence.

What I'm saying is, unless you already have a healthy financial buffer, don't ditch your job and leap into the unknown without any form of passive income behind you. Educate yourself first - both from a business perspective, and the mindset side of success. And start building your passive income streams. (Let's not forget that passive income is something that can work alongside a full-time job. It's passive, after all!) You want to get to the point where you're already earning money from investments or businesses - or, at the very least, are supremely confident that you will be making money *very* soon.

Calculated confidence, calculated risk. That's what we're talking about.

And I get that risk means different things to different people. You might never have done what I did when I was in my twenties and left my lucrative job. That's okay, we all have our own attitude to risk. Part of educating yourself might involve assessing your own risk tolerance and learning how to push your risk boundaries (where appropriate).

Education really is the key to unlocking the confidence to leave the rat race behind for good. Because confidence comes from feeling prepared. Let 'education not entertainment' become your new favourite mantra. Repeat it to yourself. I get so frustrated when I see people who are desperate to escape the rate race, but they spend their evening vegging on the sofa. They could be spending even just an hour of that time doing an online course. Don't fall into that trap yourself. Use your time wisely.

A FEW WORDS ON RAISING CONFIDENT KIDS

Anyone can learn to be more confident, but confidence certainly comes more easily if you were raised to be confident. People always say to me, 'Oh, it's alright for you, you're naturally confident.' But the truth is I was raised to be confident. And I'm so grateful for that. It's why my wife and I work at teaching our children to be confident.

We have to work a little harder at it with our son, who's four years old at the time of writing. He's definitely the shiest of our three children, whereas the two girls are brimming with confidence. So we encourage him in all the ways I've described so far in this chapter, using the tips that any adult can use to grow their confidence. For example, we encourage him to step outside of his comfort zone (like going to football club), and if he makes a mistake at something, we tell him it's okay to mess up and have a laugh when we get things wrong. We can see it paying off, little by little.

You might be wondering why I'm talking about raising confident kids in a book about becoming a millionaire. Because one of my favourite parts of being an Extraordinary Millionaire is, frankly, raising extraordinary children - children who see their parents following a different path in life, and who feel confident to one day follow their own path to wealth, freedom and an extraordinary life. Being an Extraordinary Millionaire is a family affair, and I could so easily have called this book *The Extraordinary Millionaire Family*.

So when I see children clinging onto their parents (and sometimes, parents clinging onto their children), I'm baffled. When I see parents doing everything for their children - ordering their food for them, asking questions of other adults for them, managing their homework, you name it - I'm baffled. I wonder how that child will grow up and find the confidence to step out on their own.

I also hear a lot of parents describe parenting as 'winging it'. You know, the old 'nobody knows what they're doing when it comes to parenting' line of thought. Respectfully, I have to disagree. We can learn to parent children in a way that instils self-belief. It's our duty, actually. So if you're not sure how best to instil confidence in your children, read a book on the subject. Take that time, just as you would with any other skill in this book.

To whet your appetite, here are my biggest tips for raising confident children:

- **Show them what confidence looks like.** Even if you're not feeling super-confident on the inside, model a confident, optimistic exterior for your children. Again, this doesn't mean you should act like you never get anything wrong - just don't dwell on your flaws.
- **Encourage them to try new activities (not just the things they're good at).** It's great when your kid excels at something, but it's also good for them to try things that they're not so confident or adept at. It's all part of learning.
- **Let them make their own mistakes.** Confident, happy and successful people don't let a fear of failure stop them - because they know that if they do fail, they'll pick themselves up and dust themselves off. It's a valuable lesson to learn, and the earlier your children learn it, the better. So let them learn through a process of trying and failing, with your gentle support and encouragement to back them up.
- **Make them accountable.** Don't do everything for your kids, basically. Our four-year-old fetches his own drinks (in fact, he has done since he was two) and tidies up after himself when he's been playing. And our older girls pitch in with things like kitchen tasks and looking after their little brother - as well as taking responsibility for their school work, of course.

- **Reward effort, not results.** Remember when we talked about the fixed mindset and growth mindset in Chapter 14? It's really worth learning more about this and applying it to how you talk to your children. One of the characteristics of a growth mindset is to reward effort, not results. So when your child does well in their SATs, don't say something like 'Well done, you're so clever,' - which reinforces the notion that you're either good at something or you're not - say something like, 'Well done, you worked to achieve that'. And if the outcome wasn't what they wanted, still celebrate the effort they put in.
- **Encourage them to set their own goals.** Remember in Chapter 1 when my daughter and I were updating our dream boards? It's good for kids to set their own goals - big and small - and then learn how to achieve them by breaking them down into smaller steps. At the same time, they'll also learn how to connect to their passion and pinpoint what they really want. And as we all know, achieving even small goals can deliver a big confidence boost.
- **Show them love.** Yes, my wife and I give our children quite a lot of freedom to make their own mistakes and learn for themselves what works and what doesn't. But this is balanced by an enormous amount of love and support. It's like a safety net - they're confident enough to try new things, safe in the knowledge that we'll always be there for them.

WHERE ARE YOU GOING FROM HERE?

We're nearly at the end of our journey, you and I. But before we move onto our final chapter, let me ask you one more question: will you stay a Rat Racer forever, or do you have the confidence to step out of that lane? I hope it's the latter. I hope this book has inspired you to build your own path to becoming an Extraordinary Millionaire and building an extraordinary, abundant life for you and your loved ones. I hope it's given you the confidence to try. Take it from me, it's worth it.

CONFIDENCE LESSONS FROM THE RAT RACER AND THE EXTRAORDINARY MILLIONAIRE

- The Rat Racer might mistake confidence for taking a wild leap into the unknown - quitting their job without any preparation, for example.
- But the Extraordinary Millionaire knows that confidence comes from being well-prepared. They take time to educate themselves and start building passive income before they take that leap.
- Exhausted after a busy working day, the Rat Racer wants to entertain themselves. They flop on the sofa and binge the latest Netflix offering.
- The Extraordinary Millionaire knows that successful people prioritise education over entertainment. They make time for continual learning - even if it's just an educational YouTube video before watching an episode of their favourite show.
- The Rat Racer thinks confidence is something you either have or don't have.
- The Extraordinary Millionaire knows anyone can work to build confidence, through practices like visualisation, mindfulness, positive affirmations, stepping outside their comfort zone, learning to fail, to name a few.
- The Rat Racer may work on their own confidence, while teaching their children to be risk averse and afraid of new things.
- The Extraordinary Millionaire knows that one of the best things about being an Extraordinary Millionaire is teaching your children to build their own extraordinary, abundant life. But to chart their own course requires confidence. Therefore, the Extraordinary Millionaire is constantly working to raise confident children.

Before I leave you, let's pull everything we've learned together into one final chapter and see how the Extraordinary Millionaire is all about working smart, not working hard.

Chapter 16

Working Smart, Not Hard

My oldest daughter, now a teenager, was doing a school project on people who had changed the world: Charles Darwin, Marie Curie, Mahatma Gandhi, Rosa Parks, Nelson Mandela and so on. And more recently, the likes of Mark Zuckerberg and Elon Musk. Love them or loathe them, there's no doubt that these tech billionaires are changing the world we live in – Zuckerberg by moving social interactions online, and Musk by pioneering electric car technology and commercial space flight, amongst other things.

'So what characteristics do all these extraordinary people have in common?' I asked my daughter.

She thought for a moment. 'They're wise . . . And they take action to make the world they imagine in their head a reality.'

'Brilliant,' I said. 'And they're probably pretty confident, as well, right? They believe in their own abilities?'

She nodded, then added, 'And they worked really hard.'

'What does that look like, working hard?'

She answered without hesitation. 'Probably putting in lots of hours. Did you know that Elon Musk works about 100 hours a week?' Her tone was a combination of wonder and bewilderment.

'I did know that,' I smiled. 'What do you think of that?'

'I'm not sure,' she said. 'I guess it's just what he has to do to get everything done?'

'But you know that some people are also just workaholics, right? They put all their energy into their working life at the expense of, you know, the rest of life. I'm not saying Elon Musk is a workaholic. I don't know if he is or not. But I do know he doesn't *have* to work that many hours. He chooses to.'

She thought about this, then asked, 'How many hours do you work a week?'

'Depends on the week and what's going on at work. Some weeks I'll do a regular 40-hour week – regular as in that's what most full-time people do, not Elon Musk. Other weeks I'll maybe do half that, say four hours a day or something. And during the school holidays, I'll try and just do an hour first thing so I can have the rest of the day with you guys. So, 40 hours a week at the very most. And we're doing alright aren't we?' I gestured beyond the patio to the leafy woodland surrounding us. 'I mean, this will do, won't it?'

She laughed in that *Dad, you're such an idiot* way that kids do. 'Yeah, but you're not going to change the world, are you?'

'Maybe I don't want to change the whole world, just the world of wealth creation. Maybe I'm happy having a big impact on a few people in my corner of the world. You guys, your mum, our wider family, the people I work with and the investors that I teach. That's good enough for me. And besides, even if I did want to change the whole world - even if *you* want to change the world - you don't have to drive yourself into exhaustion to do it. I don't subscribe to that notion that you have to work all hours in the day to be a super-successful person . . . But what do you think? What do you want for your future self?'

She shrugged, 'I don't want to work any more than I have to. I'd rather have time for travelling to cool places and socialising and making beautiful art. I want to be travelling as much as I can.'

'Good girl,' I smiled. 'That's the right idea. And you can do all that and still succeed in whatever way you want.'

'Sounds like a plan,' she said, in a totally nonchalant teenage way. Then she put her headphones in and went back to her school work, leaving me alone with the evening birdsong.

DO YOU REALLY WANT TO BE ELON MUSK?

'Nobody ever changed the world on 40 hours a week,' according to Elon Musk. In fact, Musk has said - and a lot of highly successful business leaders agree with him - that you need to be pulling 80-100-hour weeks. (Musk himself reportedly works up to 120 hours a week.) Anything less than 80 hours and you'll never amount to anything.

Excuse my French, but that's bullshit. I just don't want to succeed that way. I don't understand why anyone would.

True, when I was a much younger man, I quite fancied myself becoming a billionaire mogul like Elon Musk. But while it's a nice idea, having billions and flying around in a private jet, the reality is I don't want to be Elon Musk, working 20 hours a day, six days a week. I want to be successful and I only want to work eight hours a day, four or five days a week, *at the very most*. And that's only because I want to actively grow my businesses. If I was happy to just sit back and let my income-producing assets keep ticking along, I could very easily go down to one hour a day and watch the income keep flowing in.

But even though I'm still in the growth phase of my business journey – and that still excites me and drives me forward – I only want to work *hard enough*, and no more than that.

And it is possible to do that. I'm a successful person with thriving businesses and a multi-million-pound property portfolio, and my working week is no more than 40 hours max. Most weeks, it's a good deal less than that. I enjoy choice, freedom and my family, and that's my goal.

Okay, fine, I'm not going to invent something that changes the world. But who cares? I'm perfectly happy leaving that to the Elon Musks of this world. Good luck to them.

So as we come to the end of this journey together, I want you to think about what success means to you. Are you really looking to become the next Elon Musk and rank amongst the world's richest people? Or are you looking to be financially independent, to not have to work for your money, to never have to worry about money again, and to allow your children to build a similarly abundant life for themselves?

I know which one I'd prefer.

Assuming you too want the latter – financial independence rather than tech billionaire levels of wealth – I'm here to tell you that you can do it. You can do it on less than 40 hours a week. And you can do it regardless of where you're currently at in life. Admittedly, I've been working at this since my twenties and had built up to a very healthy level of passive income by my forties. But even if you're in your forties or fifties now, you can still absolutely achieve, say, a £10 million property portfolio and still be in that top 1% of UK earners - without running yourself into the ground. I believe that's doable for you. Even if you're in your sixties, you can still make it into that top 1%.

But you'll have to work smart.

WHAT DOES WORKING SMART LOOK LIKE?

Working smart is effectively what this whole book is about. It's using the mindset and wellness strategies from Part I to stay happy and set your mind (and body) up for success. It's also using the financial and entrepreneurial lessons from Part II to build passive income streams and winning business relationships.

It's managing your day efficiently, using all of the techniques in this book, and not overworking yourself.

So, working smart includes:

- Setting clear goals and taking action towards them.
- Using visualisation to breathe life into those goals and build a sense of certainty that you *will* achieve them.
- Living with abundance and the law of attraction in mind. Because what you put out you get back.
- Using affirmations and gratitude to shift your mindset to a more positive place.
- Using mindfulness and meditation techniques to tune into the here and now, and calm your mind in this busy, busy world.
- Looking after your physical health and wellness, and making sure you prioritise sleep.
- Investing time, money and effort in your continual education.
- Building a daily habit of success-boosting routines that keep you on the path towards your goals.

- Rethinking your attitude to money, and learning to *make* money rather than earn money.
- Investing in income-producing assets (which could be a business, or a physical asset) that deliver regular passive income for little work.
- Using that passive income as a strategic way to escape the rat race for good.
- Surrounding yourself with smart, inspiring people - and building a Black Book Team of your own so you can outsource tasks to experts and stop trying to do everything yourself. And, crucially, so that your business can function without you.
- Seeking out win-win relationships that allow you to reach your goals while also giving others what they want.
- Adopting a growth mindset that allows you to stop fearing failure - because failure is a natural part of learning and success.
- Building your confidence, so that you can manifest your abundant life without being held back by naysayers.
- And when the working day is done, choosing education over entertainment.

THE IMPORTANCE OF TAKING TIME OUT

I love what I do, but I also love taking time away from what I do - whether it's an impromptu midweek minibreak or going away for the whole school holidays. And I can do that because my business is able to function without me. I know my awesome team can handle the day-to-day admin, projects and property management stuff because *they already do.*

As I described in Chapter 12, my role in the business is more strategic. I'm not knee-deep in the minutia - I'm taking a broader view on how to grow my wealth, work with bigger investors, find amazing property opportunities, and create content for people like you. It may sound counter-intuitive but taking time away from the business really helps me gain that birds-eye view. Partly because I'm away from everyday routines and have the headspace to think about things like goals and strategies, and partly because getting away from it all energises me and gets my creative juices flowing.

Obviously, I'm not saying you should be locking yourself away in your hotel room to strategise on your business. Just that time away from work is a great thing, and it can be a wonderful opportunity to get re-inspired as you relax by the pool.

Here are a few ways that holidays actually help me to work smart:

- I'll read inspiring books (especially autobiographies) or catch up on educational podcasts that I love.
- I might learn a fun skill that I've never tried before. On honeymoon in Las Vegas, I got into brain training in a big way. As I soaked up the sunshine, I experimented with a new memory technique and that's how I ended up memorising the first 200 digits of Pi! If that sounds too geeky for you, activities like surfing or diving or learning to cook the local cuisine can help you stretch out your mental (and maybe even physical) muscles.
- I disengage from work emails, phone calls, meetings and, to a large extent, social media. Okay, I might need to touch base with a few things, depending on what's going on back at home, but I get it out of the way first thing and then I leave work behind for the rest of the day.
- And perhaps most importantly, I let myself daydream. I think back to my business and personal goals (and maybe add some new ones as well). This reminds me why I do what I do, and I come back to work raring to go.

All things considered, I probably come up with my best ideas when I'm on holiday or on a fishing trip, because my mind has the space to breathe and dream. So don't do yourself a disservice by skipping time away from work, or by taking work with you.

READY TO BECOME AN EXTRAORDINARY MILLIONAIRE?

Let me formally welcome you to the life of an Extraordinary Millionaire. Because as I said at the very start of this book, I was a millionaire in my head long before I ever became one on paper. You can be too, starting today. Isn't that cool? You can just start thinking of yourself as a millionaire, and start putting these techniques into practice today. Just start, now. And prepare to be amazed at the effect that shifting your mindset and changing how you think about money - and starting to take action towards your goals - can have.

An extraordinary, abundant life awaits you. Whatever that looks like to you. To me, sitting here writing these last few words, I feel abundance all around me. It's in the walls of my office yurt, and the woodland beyond that I willed into existence with the law of attraction. It's in the shrieks of delight as my children play in that woodland, and in knowing that they see a different path in life than the rat race. It's in choosing to work today because I want to, and taking the entire summer holidays off to be with family in Holland. It's in having choices in general. It's in the freedom I've built for myself and my loved ones.

Now it's time for me to hand the reins over to you. Are you going to build a similar life of freedom and choices for yourself?

I mean, what do you have to lose? As I've said in this book, I'm not advocating immediately quitting your job and jumping ship into financial uncertainty. You want this to be a calculated move, not an unnecessarily risky move. So start working on your education and working towards passive income first.

If you do it that way - building some passive income alongside your day job (for now) - it's not even that risky. Certainly not compared to staying in your rat race lane and committing to a life of working for money.

Working to make other people rich is the far riskier choice, don't you think?

And now, if you'll excuse me, I'm off to have a go on the zip line.

www.ingramcontent.com/pod-product-compliance
Lightning Source LLC
Chambersburg PA
CBHW070028100426
42740CB00013B/2623